AF574400

Silence, Space and Absence in Conrad's Works

John G. Peters

Silence, Space and Absence in Conrad's Works

Western and Non-Western Worlds

palgrave
macmillan

John G. Peters
Department of English
University of North Texas
Denton, TX, USA

ISBN 978-3-031-44909-3 ISBN 978-3-031-44910-9 (eBook)
https://doi.org/10.1007/978-3-031-44910-9

This Palgrave Macmillan imprint is published by the registered company Springer Nature Switzerland AG.
The registered company address is: Gewerbestrasse 11, 6330 Cham, Switzerland

Paper in this product is recyclable.

"Before the Congo I was just a mere animal."
Joseph Conrad

For my sister, Virginia

Preface and Acknowledgments

Throughout this book, a separate Works Cited page follows each chapter rather than a comprehensive Works Cited page following the entire book. Three unspaced periods signal my ellipses for material I have omitted from quotations. Three spaced periods signal ellipses appearing in the original quoted matter. I have silently changed instances in quoted material that call for different capitalization or punctuation to fit the surrounding sentence rather than using square brackets to signal such changes. Throughout I have gravitated toward recent editions of Conrad's works based upon the first English edition, which, despite some house styling, represents I believe Conrad's final determination for the text at the time of publication. Where such editions are unavailable, I have used the Cambridge University Press edition of Conrad's works. Where neither is available, I have used the uniform Doubleday/Dent edition.

I am grateful for the helpful comments of colleagues in writing this book. In particular, I would like to thank Bruce Bond, who is always willing to listen to my arguments and ideas and provide insightful responses, and to Hunt Hawkins for sharing resources with me. I am also grateful to the faculty of the Department of English at the University of South Alabama that provided helpful feedback to a guest lecture on the space of the West and non-West in Conrad's African tales, which formed part of the basis for my discussion of those stories. As always, I am thankful for the support I continually receive from my department and family and to the interlibrary loan department at the University of North Texas for their tireless efforts to find obscure materials for my research. An earlier version of part of this book appeared in *Texas Studies in Literature and Language*, and I appreciate their allowing me to incorporate it here.

Denton, TX, USA John G. Peters

Contents

Abbreviations

AF	*Almayer's Folly*
AG	*The Arrow of Gold*
AW	"Autocracy and War"
BD	"Because of the Dollars"
BM	"The Black Mate"
CL	*The Collected Letters of Joseph Conrad*
CP	"The Crime of Partition"
D	*The Duel*
F	*Falk*
ET	*The End of the Tether*
FSI	"Freya of the Seven Isles"
GSE	"Geography and Some Explorers"
HD	*Heart of Darkness*
K	"Karain"
L	"The Lagoon"
LJ	*Lord Jim*
NN	*The Nigger of the "Narcissus"*
N	*Nostromo*
OI	*An Outcast of the Islands*
OP	"An Outpost of Progress"
PR	*A Personal Record*
R	*The Rescue*
SA	*The Secret Agent*
SS	"The Secret Sharer"
SL	*The Shadow-Line*
S	*The Sisters*
Ta	"The Tale"

Ty	*Typhoon*
UWE	*Under Western Eyes*
V	*Victory*
WS	"The Warrior's Soul"
Y	"Youth"

CHAPTER 1

Conrad's Colonial Spaces

Abstract This chapter presents a review of literature of important commentary on Conrad and colonialism and situates this book's argument within the context of the existing conversation.

Keywords Joseph Conrad • Colonialism • Chinua Achebe • Imperialism

This book will consider the relationship between silence, space, and absence in Joseph Conrad's works. More especially, it will consider these elements in light of the relationship between Conrad's depiction of Western and non-Western space. In his writings, Conrad presents these spaces as both distinct and indistinct: his narrators initially describing them as distinct, even antithetical to one another, but eventually revealing how these distinctions dissolve. By way of introduction, to address the issue of Conrad's Western and non-Western spaces adequately, it is first necessary to understand the relationship between Conrad's Western and non-Western worlds, in other words, the conversation concerning Conrad and colonialism.[1]

[1] Parts of this introduction draw somewhat from sections of my *Joseph Conrad's Critical Reception*.

J. G. Peters, *Silence, Space and Absence in Conrad's Works*,
https://doi.org/10.1007/978-3-031-44910-9_1

Early Commentary

For the last fifty years, Conrad's depiction of the colonial world has attracted considerable conversation. In fact, during that time, no other subject has so frequently engendered debate. This trend is unsurprising considering how much of Conrad's work is set in the colonial world. What is surprising is that prior to the 1970s, Conrad's relationship to the colonial world drew little attention.

Hugh Clifford, in a well-known review for the *Singapore Free Press* (1898), was perhaps the first to focus on Conrad's actual depiction of the colonial world, famously contending that Conrad's Malays did not at all resemble actual Malays.[2] Somewhat in the wake of Clifford's concerns, Florence Clemens's 1937 dissertation, *Conrad's Malaysian Fiction* (finally published by Brill in 2022), was the only extended study of Conrad's colonial world until Robert Lee's discussion of the topic in his *Conrad's Colonialism* (1969). Neither, however, reflects the conversation about Conrad and colonialism that has encompassed commentators during the last half century. Clemens's work is valuable but largely historical, identifying Conrad's sources, his use of history and geography, and his relationship to other chroniclers of the region such as Clifford, Frank Swettenham, and Alfred Russel Wallace. In contrast, Lee considers the issue of colonialism itself – but from the vantage of the colonizer, affirming what Rudyard Kipling termed "the white man's burden" and arguing that Conrad also affirmed that philosophy.

Prior to the 1970s, even shorter studies on the subject were largely non-existent. A notable exception is Arnold Kettle's "The Greatness of Joseph Conrad" (1948), which considers colonial issues in *Nostromo* (1904) in light of Marxist thinking. Kettle argued that Conrad was the sole author of his time to take an honest look at the problems of imperialism. At the same time, Kettle initiates a thread that has continued in successive discussions of Conrad and the colonial world to the present day: that Conrad was both a critic of colonialism but also its subtle proponent.

[2] Throughout, I use the term Malay generically (as Conrad often did) to refer to regions and peoples of the Malay and Philippine archipelagos. The people of this region were, of course, of diverse backgrounds and cultures. However, since Conrad is rarely specific in his geographical settings regarding this region, and actually resisted attempts to pin down where his works were set (*e.g.*, CL 7: 456-57), it is often impossible to determine whether a character is Bugis, Dyak, Macassar, Sulu, or a member of one of the hundreds of other communities of this region.

Two other commentators during this early period made brief forays into this field. Eloise Knapp Hay's *The Political Novels of Joseph Conrad* (1963) was among the first to consider Conrad's critique of colonialism as an element of his politics. Hay notes that part of the backdrop for the writing of *Heart of Darkness* (1899), for example, was the Boer War, which marked one of the few times Conrad expressed criticism of British foreign policy. Hay also includes among Conrad's political novels *The Rescue* (1920) because of its focus on the relationship between East and West during the colonial period. Avrom Fleishman's *Conrad's Politics* (1967) supplements the existing discussion surrounding Conrad's views of colonialism, arguing that Conrad depicted colonial intervention as leading consistently to social disorder, both for the colonizer and for the colonized.

Raymond Williams is also among the early commentators on colonialism in Conrad. Like Kettle, he considers the issue in view of Marxist philosophy. In his *The English Novel from Dickens to Lawrence* (1970), Williams argues that the issues of isolation and struggle that many commentators have identified in Conrad's writings are social and not individual issues and are directly related to humanity's attempt to survive within social systems of value. In particular, Williams focuses on *Heart of Darkness* and its engagement with the colonial activities in the Congo, despite the dearth of contemporary commentary on the issue. Similarly, Jean Franco's "The Limits of the Liberal Imagination" (1975), picks up on Kettle's response to colonialism in *Nostromo*. Franco argues that Conrad is primarily interested in how national ideals foster colonialism while concealing their actual nature from those involved. But Conrad could not break through the barriers of liberal imagination that questioned contemporary materialism and saw as inevitable Western domination of Latin America. While critical of colonialism, Conrad approves of such Latin Americans as Avellanos and Ribeira, who are amenable to Western influence. In contrast, he strongly critiques the Monteros and other anti-European revolutionaries, representing them as politically immature and implying the need for Western intervention. Despite these limitations, Franco considers *Nostromo* a perceptive and devastating account of imperialism in the vein of J. A. Hobson's view of nationalism intensified by imperialism. Terry Eagleton, in *Criticism & Ideology* (1976), follows Kettle and Williams, contending that in *Heart of Darkness* Conrad rejects Belgian imperialist exploitation but believes that imperialism based on ideals (as in the merchant marine service) resolves the conflict between romantic nationalism and colonial realities. In this way, Conrad both rejects and reinforces imperialist ideas.

The first extended discussion of Conrad's depiction of colonialism was D. C. R. A. Goonetilleke's *Developing Countries in British Fiction* (1977), a book predominantly about Conrad. Like Kettle and others, Goonetilleke recognizes that Conrad both transcends his cultural perspectives but is also a product of them. Goonetilleke suggests that Conrad's depictions of Malays and Chinese lack much of the conventional Western biases, but at the same time (following Clifford), Conrad also reveals his ignorance of such cultures.

Chinua Achebe's Response to Conrad

While Goonetilleke opened the door to a postcolonial perspective of Conrad's colonialism, Chinua Achebe's landmark essay "An Image of Africa" (1977) almost single-handedly turned critical attention toward Conrad's colonial views. Achebe's argument is twofold. First, he contends that Conrad reinforces Western stereotypes of Africans in his depiction of African characters, in effect dehumanizing his Africans. Achebe also contends that Conrad perpetuates long-standing racial prejudices and as such reveals himself to be a racist. Second, Achebe argues that because the novel dehumanizes Africans it ought not to be considered a great work of literature. No single commentary on Conrad has attracted as much response as Achebe's article, both from those affirming his views and from those rejecting them.

Several subsequent responses are indicative of the conversation that Achebe generated. Francis Singh, for example, in "The Colonialist Bias of *Heart of Darkness*" (1978), reinforces Achebe's accusations, acknowledging that Conrad is critical of colonialism but that despite Conrad's criticism he nevertheless betrays Western biases toward Africans, locating "the source of the psychological heart of darkness in Africans" (44), expressing "only superficial" sympathy for the oppressed blacks (45), and finding "blacks to be morally inferior" to Marlow and those like him (46). In this way, Singh supplements Achebe's views.

Other contemporary commentators disagree with Achebe. Hunt Hawkins's "Conrad's Critique of Imperialism in *Heart of Darkness*" (1979) responds indirectly to Achebe. He contends that Conrad criticized imperialism, both in his obvious contempt for Belgian colonialism but also in a more subtle critique of British colonialism. Hawkins further suggests that Conrad opposed colonialism because it disrupted indigenous cultures. Cedric Watts (1983) enacted a more direct attack on Achebe's position ("'A bloody racist': About Achebe's View of Conrad"), countering each of Achebe's complaints. Watts disputes that Conrad dehumanizes the Africans, reinforces white supremacy, or allows Africans no speech but only rudimentary sounds.

Patrick Brantlinger in "*Heart of Darkness*: Anti-Imperialism, Racism, or Impressionism?" (1985), navigates a middle course between Achebe and Watts, contending that *Heart of Darkness* both criticizes imperialism and racism and is itself imperialist and racist, impressionism being the connecting cable between the two. Brantlinger especially emphasizes Conrad's condemnation of idealistic imperialist propaganda, associating it with idolatry. However, while condemning imperialism, Conrad links the savagery of Western imperialism to African savagery, thereby revealing an underlying racism. Brantlinger argues that in the end Conrad's critique of empire is not nihilistic but conservative, as he longs for true faith and laments the loss of adventure and the death of chivalry.

This debate has been a consistent trend since that time, amounting to scores of articles and book chapters. In fact, Peter Edgerly Firchow (2000) wrote an entire monograph on Conrad's depiction of Africa (*Envisioning Africa*), roughly a third of which engages with Achebe. Firchow disagrees with Achebe's accusation that Conrad dehumanizes his African characters and argues that Conrad was not depicting Africa itself but only an image of Africa. Even as recently as 2022, Trung Le entered the Conrad and Achebe debate, arguing for a middle course between opponents and proponents of Achebe's position ("An Appeal to the Other in Us").[3]

Continuing Commentary on Colonialism

Other commentators have, of course, made other important contributions to the conversation concerning Conrad and colonialism. Like the critical conversation specifically surrounding Chinua Achebe's critique of *Heart of Darkness*, the broader conversation surrounding colonialism in Conrad has flourished since it became a prominent point of emphasis. Among the more notable commentators writing in the aftermath of Goonetilleke and Achebe are Benita Parry, Edward W. Said, and Christopher GoGwilt. For

[3] Although dated 2018, volume 50, issue 1 of *Conradiana* (in which Le's article appeared) was not actually published until 2022.

instance, Benita Parry, in her *Conrad and Imperialism* (1983) asserts that Conrad exposes colonialism's abuses and tunnel vision but also exoticizes non-Westerners and endorses racial solidarity, Western codes, and Western moral standards. Regarding *Heart of Darkness*, for instance, Parry contends that Conrad denounces imperialist ideology while supporting its idealist values; consequently, his political protest is muted. Parry sees a similar pattern of rejection but simultaneous affirmation of colonialism in such works as *Nostromo*, *The Rescue*, and *Lord Jim* (1900).

In *Culture and Imperialism* (1993), Edward W. Said presents another view of Conrad as both opponent and proponent of colonialism by discussing two visions of imperialism in *Heart of Darkness*. The first is a conventional Western view, which saw itself as superior to the colonial world, a world forever inferior to the West. In the second vision, Conrad does not posit a complete alternative to imperialism, nor does he present a world where colonial subjects are capable of independence. However, even if Conrad cannot imagine a postcolonial world, he does imagine the imperial world ending. Ultimately, Said sees Conrad as a product of his time: he could envision the conquering and controlling aspect of imperialism, but he could not envision that imperialism should be abolished so that colonial subjects could then lead lives free from imperial control.

Christopher GoGwilt's 1995 *The Invention of the West* takes yet another approach to Conrad's colonialism. GoGwilt contends that the very concept of a unified West was a social construct that the West then used to justify controlling the non-Western world. GoGwilt looks at Conrad's own conception of the West, arguing that he both supports and rejects a constructed West. In Conrad's early writings, GoGwilt sees the cultural collision between Malays and Europeans in the imperialist context revealing the discontinuity of European identity and the distortion of the idea of the West. In *Lord Jim*, for example, the novel embodies a shift from a nineteenth-century Orientalism to a twentieth-century concept of the West.

Other commentators have also contributed productively to this conversation and continue to do so. John A. McClure, in his *Kipling* & Conrad (1981), contends that Conrad questioned romanticized colonialism. For Conrad, colonialism corrupts and augments rather than alleviates suffering. McClure argues that European colonizers in the Malay novels consistently destroy rather than improve the colonial world. Even those who, like Jim and Lingard, wish to be agents of benevolence end by enslaving indigenous peoples and damaging their societies. Nor does the situation change in Africa, where in *Heart of Darkness* McClure insists colonial exploitation is even more blatant and brutal. Of *Nostromo*, McClure argues that economic colonialism destroys Latin American nations, and, rather than liberating them, it enslaves them. Finally, McClure concludes that despite Conrad's general critique of colonialism, his own aristocratic background sometimes blinded him to the limits of his criticism.

Henryk Zins, in *Joseph Conrad in Africa* (1982), diverges from the conventional conversation asserting Conrad's bifurcated response the issue and defends Conrad against charges of racism and pro-colonialism. To do so, Zins invokes Conrad's Polish background, arguing that his experience in occupied Poland left him critical of colonialism. Zins also looks at Conrad's experience in England and asserts that his politics were on the liberal rather than the conservative side, counter to, for example, Irving Howe's view of Conrad's politics (*e.g.*, 79). Zins further argues that Conrad's views on Africa and Africans are much more forward thinking than those of most of his contemporaries and that Conrad consistently critiques colonialism.

Like so many other commentaries, Chris Bongie's *Exotic Memories* (1991) posits a tension in Conrad's works between a criticism and rationalization of colonial activities, but in making this argument, Bongie focuses on the link between exoticism and colonialism, suggesting that Conrad longed for the exotic world of the past where individuality was possible, as one encountered it in the new and undiscovered. Bongie contents that Conrad was repulsed by the modern world where individuality was increasingly non-existent, but Bongie also sees Conrad's views regarding individualism as closely linked to his attitudes toward colonialism.

An important development arose during this time involving a connection between Conrad's colonialism and issues of gender. Heliéna Krenn, Padmini Mongia, and Marianna Torgovnick are representative of this permutation. Like Zins, Heliéna Krenn defends Conrad's representation of the colonial world. In her *Conrad's Lingard Trilogy* (1990), Krenn argues that Conrad does not exhibit racist or sexist tendencies and instead critiques these social norms of his day. She sees Conrad as critical of the racist and sexist views of Almayer, Willems, and Lingard and notes the admirable qualities of Dain Maroola, Nina, Hassim, and Immada, for example. Padmini Mongia moves in a somewhat different direction. She argues for the place of *Lord Jim* and *Heart of Darkness* among the works of adventure writers of the Victorian and Edwardian eras such as H. Rider Haggard, Robert Louis Stevenson, and Rudyard Kipling. Within this adventure novel genre, indigenous women play a small part but can have a large impact, demarcating the male world but also representing the threatening and seductive. Marianna Torgovnick's *Gone Primitive* (1990) also ties gender and colonialism even more closely, contending that *Heart of Darkness* and *Lord Jim* hold out the promise of an objective view of Africa, but end by reinforcing conventional views of the female and primitive, with both remaining at the mercy of masculine fantasy.

More recent extended voices in this conversation on Conrad and colonialism include Robert Hampson, Agnes S. K. Yeow, Terry Collits, and Stephen Ross. Robert Hampson's *Cross-Cultural Encounters in Joseph Conrad's Malay Fiction* (2000) considers Conrad and the colonial world, specifically focusing on his Malay writings. Hampson argues that these works come out of Conrad's personal experience and out of a historical pattern of Western constructs of the Malay world. He further suggests that Conrad was aware of this construct and routinely deconstructed it. In the process of discussing Conrad's Malay writings, Hampson uncovers problems with Western constructs of the non-Western world, as he examines various ways Westerners attempt to represent the Other. For Hampson, in all these permutations, as Conrad attempts to write Malaysia, he comes to represent Europe to a progressively greater degree through the lens of cross-cultural encounters with Malaysia.

Like Hampson, Agnes S. K. Yeow's *Conrad's Eastern Vision* (2009), considers Conrad's Malay fiction, but Yeow's overarching interest rests in the relationship between historical and fictional representation. A dialogue arises among differing purveyors of truth: history and art (each representing different truths). This results in an open-ended depiction of the East, where culture, civilization, subjectivity, and racial difference are deconstructed, with Conrad's vision of the East appearing as a hallucinated mirage. At the same time, Conrad represents a vision that carries the illusion of truth. After establishing the nature of Conrad's vision of the East, Yeow then considers his construction of Malay religious and political identity (particularly in light of *Lord Jim*), arguing that Conrad shows an astute understanding of politics, resulting in a subtle criticism of colonial indirect rule and a critique of Western assumptions of racial and moral superiority.

Stephen Ross's *Conrad and Empire* (2004) moves in yet another direction as he investigates globalization and empire, with imperialism resulting from globalization. Ross argues that Conrad's fiction explores how global capitalism replaces the traditional concept of the nation-state, and he considers how this affects Conrad's characters. Ross concludes by asserting that despite Conrad's bleak commentary on the modern world, a glimpse of affirmation remains: while rejecting strong idealism and unwavering faith, Conrad affirms an ethics of contingency that averts nihilism.

Finally, Terry Collits's *Postcolonial Conrad* (2005) approaches the relationship between Conrad and colonialism from yet a different angle, arguing for Conrad's less ambivalent and more critical view of colonialism. In discussing *Victory* (1915), for example, Collits reassesses its literary quality and argues that it narrates the failures of skeptical philosophy and European colonialism. Collits disagrees with the novel's defenders who emphasize its allegorical and romance elements. Collits focuses instead on the prominent roles Wang and Lena perform and contends that Conrad critiques imperialism by leaving Wang alone victorious at the novel's close.

As I argued at the outset of this chapter, I have presented this extended review of literature because of the extended conversation that exists concerning Conrad's colonialism. Such a review outlines the borders of the conversation that exists as the backdrop to my study of Conrad's Western and non-Western space, and even though I will be considering an ancillary aspect of this broad topic, that is the relationship between Western space and non-Western space, the larger conversation concerning Conrad and colonialism will serve as an important context for my own investigations.

References

Achebe, Chinua. "An Image of Africa." *Massachusetts Review*, vol. 18, no. 4, winter 1977, pp. 782–94.

Bongie, Chris. *Exotic Memories: Literature, Colonialism, and the Fin de Siècle*. Stanford, CA: Stanford University Press, 1991.

Brantlinger, Patrick. "*Heart of Darkness*: Anti-Imperialism, Racism, or Impressionism?" *Criticism*, vol. 27, no. 4, fall 1985, pp. 363–85.

Clemens, Florence. "Conrad's Malaysian Fiction: A New Study in Sources with an Analysis of Factual Material Involved." Ph.D. Dissertation. Ohio State University, 1937.

[Clifford, Hugh]. "The Trail of the Book-Worm: Mr. Joseph Conrad at Home and Abroad." *The Singapore Free Press*, 30 August 1898, p. 3.

Collits, Terry. *Postcolonial Conrad: Paradoxes of Empire*. New York: Routledge, 2005.

Conrad, Joseph. *The Collected Letters of Joseph Conrad*. Edited by Laurence Davies, et al, 9 vols. Cambridge: Cambridge University Press, 1983–2008.

Eagleton, Terry. *Criticism & Ideology*. London: NLB, 1976.

Firchow, Peter Edgerly. *Envisioning Africa: Racism and Imperialism in Conrad's "Heart of Darkness."* Lexington: University of Kentucky Press, 2000.
Fleishman, Avrom. *Conrad's Politics: Community and Anarchy in the Fiction of Joseph Conrad.* Baltimore, MD: Johns Hopkins University Press, 1967.
Franco, Jean. "The Limits of the Liberal Imagination: *One Hundred Years of Solitude* and *Nostromo.*" *Punto de Contacto*, vol. 1, no. 1, December 1975, pp. 4–16.
GoGwilt, Christopher. *The Invention of the West: Joseph Conrad and the Double-Mapping of Europe and Empire.* Stanford, CA: Stanford University Press, 1995.
Goonetilleke, D. C. R. A. *Developing Countries in British Fiction.* Totowa, NJ: Rowman and Littlefield, 1977.
Hampson, Robert. *Cross-Cultural Encounters in Joseph Conrad's Malay Fiction.* New York: Palgrave, 2000.
Hawkins, Hunt. "Conrad's Critique of Imperialism in *Heart of Darkness.*" *PMLA*, vol. 94, no. 2, March 1979, pp. 286–99.
Hay, Eloise Knapp. *The Political Novels of Joseph Conrad: A Critical Study.* Chicago: University of Chicago Press, 1963.
Howe, Irving. *Politics and the Novel.* New York: Horizon Books, 1957.
Kettle, Arnold. "The Greatness of Joseph Conrad." *Modern Quarterly*, n.s. vol. 3, no. 3, summer 1948, pp. 63–81.
Krenn, Heliéna. *Conrad's Lingard Trilogy: Empire, Race, and Women in the Malay Novels.* New York: Garland, 1990.
Le, Trung. "An Appeal to the Other in Us: Intimated Oppositions between Chinua Achebe and Conrad's *Heart of Darkness.*" *Conradiana*, vol. 50, no 1, spring 2018, pp. 19–55.
Lee, Robert F. *Conrad's Colonialism.* The Hague: Mouton, 1969.
McClure, John A. *Kipling & Conrad: The Colonial Fiction.* Cambridge, MA: Harvard University Press, 1981.
Mongia, Padmini. "Empire, Narrative and the Feminine in *Lord Jim* and *Heart of Darkness.*" *Contexts for Conrad.* Edited by Keith Carabine, Owen Knowles, and Wiesław Krajka. Boulder, CO: East European Monographs, 1993, pp. 135–50.
Parry, Benita. *Conrad and Imperialism: Ideological Boundaries and Visionary Frontiers.* London: Macmillan, 1983.
Peters, John G. *Joseph Conrad's Critical Reception.* Cambridge: Cambridge University Press, 2013.
Ross, Stephen. *Conrad and Empire.* Columbia: University of Missouri Press, 2004.
Said, Edward W. *Culture and Imperialism.* New York: Alfred A. Knopf, 1993.
Singh, Frances B. "The Colonialist Bias of *Heart of Darkness.*" *Conradiana*, vol. 10, no. 1, spring 1978, pp. 41–54.
Torgovnick, Marianna. *Gone Primitive: Savage Intellects, Modern Lives.* Chicago: University of Chicago Press, 1990.

Watts, Cedric. "'A bloody racist': About Achebe's View of Conrad." *Yearbook of English Studies*, vol. 13, 1983, pp. 196–209.
Williams, Raymond. *The English Novel from Dickens to Lawrence*. New York: Oxford University Press, 1970.
Yeow, Agnes S. K. *Conrad's Eastern Vision: A Vain and Floating Appearance*. New York: Palgrave Macmillan, 2009.
Zins, Henryk. *Joseph Conrad and Africa*. Nairobi: Kenya Literature Bureau, 1982.

CHAPTER 2

Silence, Sound, Space

Abstract This chapter looks at the various instances where Conrad's characters present Western space associated with sound and activity and non-Western space associated with an absence of both, describing such spaces as silent and empty.

Keywords Joseph Conrad • Silence • Sound • Space • Emptiness • Western • Non-Western

The space of Africa provided Joseph Conrad with the catalyst for a life-altering existential journey. He once told Edward Garnett, "Before the Congo I was just a mere animal" (Jean-Aubry 1: 141).[1] The illumination Conrad experienced through his engagement with the Congo runs counter to conventional cultural convictions of the West because for Conrad the Congo disseminated not ignorance but understanding, converting Conrad from a state of unknowing to one of knowing.

[1] Garnett elaborates, quoting Conrad as saying that before the Congo he had "not a thought in his head.... I was a perfect animal" (8). Compare also Conrad's comments in his "Author's Note" (1917) to *Youth: A Narrative and Two Other Stories* (1902): "*Heart of Darkness* is experience too; but it is experience pushed a little (and only very little) beyond the actual facts" (46-47) and his "Author's Note" (1919) to *Tales of Unrest* (1898): "'An Outpost of Progress' is the lightest part of the loot I carried off from Central Africa, the main portion being of course 'The Heart of Darkness'" (6).

J. G. Peters, *Silence, Space and Absence in Conrad's Works*,
https://doi.org/10.1007/978-3-031-44910-9_2

As he traveled through Africa, layers of his familiar ordered and civilized society dissolved, revealing in their stead an essential absence. Numerous characters (on both large and small scales) replicate Conrad's metamorphic expedition. Conrad transmits these transformations through the interplay between silence and space, especially in the interplay between Western and non-Western space. This book will consider those transformative experiences that result (as did Conrad's own traumatic transformation) from the collision of Western and non-Western space, encounters that force Conrad's characters to reevaluate how they weigh the world.

The association of non-Western space with silence is a common quality among the various incarnations of non-Western space that Conrad's characters encounter. Time and again, the space of the non-Western world is silent. At the same time, this silent space is also empty, whether it be the jungles of Africa, the forests of Borneo, the expanse of Russia, or the vastness of the oceans.[2] Moreover, the spatial silence in these tales appears as both literal and figurative:[3] without sound, without speech, without sense, as does its emptiness: without objects, without ethics, without reason.[4] Even space itself appears as both literal and figurative: geographical,

[2] Conrad always associated Russia with non-Western space; see, for instance, "The Crime of Partition" (CP 94) and Conrad's letters (*e.g.* CL 6: 180-81 and 207). In the conclusion to this book, I will elaborate on Conrad's view of the unique qualities of the non-Western space of Russia.

[3] Many critics have investigated various aspects of silence in Conrad's works. For example, Daniel Hannah looks at the silences in *Lord Jim* as evidence of Romantic irony in the tradition of Schlegel; Martin Ray finds the origins of Conrad's silence in the Symbolists (especially Mallarmé and Rimbaud), which provides catharsis in light of the limitations of language; and in Pascal, who connected silence with the annihilation of an author's work; Sarah Dauncey sees the silence of *Victory* as a silence of resistance against Eurocentric views (both for women and for colonial subjects); Brian Richardson investigates the workings of silence in the interaction between a bevy of Conrad's characters (*e.g.*, Alvan Hervey and his wife, Lingard and Mrs. Travers, Nostromo and Giorgio Viola, and Renouard and Felicia) and how these silences reflect posthumanism and affect the characters and the direction of these works; Daniel Melnick argues for the effect of the silence imposed by autocracy in *Under Western Eyes*; and Aaron Fogel examines the way Conrad's characters are coerced from silence to speech. See also Richard Pedot, Eric Rawson, Deborah McLeod, Sanford Pinsker, Eugene Hollahan, Margaret Sönmez, Jerry Wasserman, and Annika J. Lindskog for other views on silence in Conrad. These valuable studies provide a context for my investigations, but I am interested, in contrast, in the communicative characteristics of silence in Conrad's stories.

[4] As noted earlier, Chinua Achebe famously criticized a Western penchant in general and Conrad's penchant in particular of presenting Africa as "a place of negations" (783), even down to the lack of language among the African characters in *Heart of Darkness*: "It is clearly not part of Conrad's purpose to confer language on the 'rudimentary souls' of Africa" (786). For more on this silence, see Dorothy Trench-Bonett, Joanna Kurowska, and Myrtle Hooper, who each dialogues with Achebe's critique of this lack of language.

political, phenomenological.[5] The permutations of silence that appear in these stories all point toward a similar terminus: toward the negation of the heard, as do the permutations of emptiness, which point toward the negation of the extant. In the end, incarnations of the silent and of the empty converge at the locus of non-Western space to expose an absence in both non-Western and Western space, an absence that is more than mere silence, more than mere emptiness, but rather a universe without order, without purpose, without meaning. Conrad's characters, however, discover this state slowly; their journeys begin in an absence of sound and end in an absence of meaning, and only through their cumulative experiences in the silent and empty spaces they enter do they at last come to perceive a universe of absolute absence. At their journey's outset, though, distinctions between Western and non-Western space abound: sound opposed to silence, fullness opposed to emptiness; meaning opposed to absurdity.

"An Outpost of Progress" (1897), for example, describes a "silent river" flowing through an African space that "stretching away in all directions … lay in the eloquent silence of mute greatness" (OP 82). The narrator refers as well to "the great silence of the surrounding wilderness" (OP 92), which remains "a formidable silence" (OP 98) throughout the tale. Similarly, Marlow speaks of the Congo as an "unapproachable silence" (HD 119) and calls it "a great silence" (HD 73, 91); he remarks that "the river, the shore, the woods, were very quiet – perfectly quiet" (HD 105); and he refers to a wilderness "without a sound" (HD 78). Here and in numerous other places, these tales equate the space of Africa with silence.[6] Anne McClintock remarks of Marlow's view of the African wilderness that "what appalls Marlowe [*sic*] most of all is the refusal of the landscape to speak. … This is repeated with such frequency that silence gradually

[5] Conrad studies have produced powerful and provocative readings of Conrad and space. Con Coroneos, for example, investigates Conrad's geographical spaces, as does Katherine Isobel Baxter; Cesare Casarino, and Robert Hampson ("Spatial Stories") examine Conrad's heterotopic spaces; Harry Sewlall and Sanjay Krishnan consider Conrad's colonial spaces, while Padmini Mongia and Attie de Lange focus on Conrad's gendered colonial spaces. Other critics delve into more figurative spaces: Merry W. Pawloski looks at Conrad's gendered spaces in light of cultural space; Wesley A. Kort comments on labor and Conrad's social spaces; Joanna Mstowska examines Conrad's inner spaces; Sarah Dauncey explores Conrad's metaphysical spaces; Nathalie Martinière studies Conrad's symbolic spaces; and elsewhere, I have looked at the epistemology of space in Conrad. In contrast to these studies, I am interested in a different aspect of space: its relationship to silence and to absence and the relationship of both to Conrad's Western and non-Western worlds.

[6] See also "An Outpost of Progress" (OP 82, 92, 98) and *Heart of Darkness* (HD 86, 90, 91, 92, 93, 95, 96, and so on).

becomes the definitive attribute of the landscape" (48). Conrad also connects the silence of African space with its stillness. Allon White contends of *Heart of Darkness* that "stillness applies to both noise and movement, denoting their combined stasis" (114). However, their connection is even closer: both are absences, stillness being a clear contributing component to the silence of the wilderness.

Conrad does not limit the association of silence with the space of Africa alone; instead, he associates non-Western space in general with silence, and in so doing, like Africa, other non-Western spaces become the catalyst for the life-altering events that so many of Conrad's characters encounter, as they too replicate Conrad's transformative Congo ordeal. "Karain: A Memory" (1897), for instance, assesses of Karain's land: "The seamed hills became black shadows towering high upon a clear sky; above them the glittering confusion of stars resembled a mad turmoil stilled by a gesture; sounds ceased" (K 18). As with the description of Africa, Karain's land, located in the Philippines and isolated from the Western world and its influence, is a silent space.

Many of Conrad's tales are set in the Malay Archipelago, and their commonality is the silent space they share. "Freya of the Seven Isles" (1912) refers to an island's "low coast of virgin forests, inviolate and mute" (FSI 168), and Davidson, in "Because of the Dollars" (1914), experiences "the dumb stillness" of the land (BD 153). Similarly, *The End of the Tether* (1902) points to "the great stillness that reigned upon the coast" (ET 201; see also 202, 263, and 276). In "The Lagoon" (1897), space holds such prominence that Lawrence Graver contends that it is "the protagonist" of the story (28). The narrator says of Arsat's land, "The forests, sombre and dull, stood motionless and silent on each side of the broad stream. … In the stillness of the air every tree, every leaf, every bough, every tendril of creeper and every petal of minute blossoms seemed to have been bewitched into an immobility perfect and final" (L 155) and goes on to refer to "the breathless silence of the world" (L 156). Later, Arsat and the narrator "sat in silence before the fire. There was no sound within the house, there was no sound near them. … The land and the water slept invisible, unstirring and mute" (L 159; see also 160 and 166). Throughout Conrad's Malay tales, space begins and ends in silence.

Contributing to this state of silence in the Malay Archipelago and its environs, *Almayer's Folly* (1895) refers to the "silent sleeping coast" (AF 9), the "silent space" of Sambir (AF 134), and the "solemn and impressive silence" of its forests (AF 55), while the captain in "The Secret Sharer"

(1910) speaks of the island of Koh-ring as being "without a sound" (SS 40). In the same way, in *Lord Jim*, Marlow more than once describes Patusan as "silent" (*e.g.*, LJ 236, 292, 295, 326, 351), and *Victory* remarks, "The islands are very quiet" (V 54), as are the forests of New Guinea (V 66). *The Rescue* observes that "the coast, the shallows, the dark islets and the snowy sandbanks uncovered thus day after day were seen once more in their aspect of dumb watchfulness" (R 146), elsewhere referring to the "absolute silence" (R 151) and the "impenetrable silence" (R 244) of the land (see also R 149, 150, 167, 255, 330). The same is true of the East that Marlow first perceives in "Youth: A Narrative" (1898). As he nears the shore, "suddenly a puff of wind, a puff faint and tepid and laden with strange odors of blossoms, of aromatic wood, comes out of the still night – the first sigh of the East on my face" (Y 38-39). Marlow then elaborates on this non-Western space: "The scented obscurity of the shore was grouped into vast masses, a density of colossal clumps of vegetation, probably – mute and fantastic shapes. ... There was not a light, not a stir, not a sound. The mysterious East faced me, perfumed like a flower, silent like death, dark like a grave" (Y 39).[7] Later, when the other lifeboats reach shore, Marlow notes, "The East looked at them without a sound" (Y 42). Regardless of any sound he may encounter thereafter, its dominant state is not sound but silence.

Conrad extends this link between silence and the non-Western world to his description of the sea, routinely painting it with the color of silence. For instance, "The Black Mate" (1908) refers to "the silence brooding over the great waters" (BM 103), while the captain in *The Shadow-Line* (1917) describes the ocean as being "steeped in an infinity of silence" (SL 90) and says of it, "The brooding stillness of the world seemed sensitive to the slightest sound, like a whispering gallery" (SL 114). *The End of the Tether* extends this assessment, describing "the still, dark sea" (ET 225), as does *The Rescue*, which refers to "the dumb testimony of the sea" (R 121). Conrad himself, in *A Personal Record* (1912), speaks of "the great silence of the sea" (PR 75), and the narrator of *The Nigger of the "Narcissus"* (1897) remarks of "the sea that stretched away on all sides [and] merged into the illimitable silence of all creation" (NN 237). The captain of "The Secret Sharer" concurs, suggesting of the sea surrounding his ship that

[7] Compare also Marlow's assessment of the non-Westerners he observes: "I saw brown, bronze, yellow faces, the black eyes, the glitter, the color of an Eastern crowd. And all these beings stared without a murmur, without a sigh, without a movement" (Y 41-42).

"nothing moved, nothing lived, not a canoe on the water, not a bird in the air, not a cloud in the sky" (SS 8) and later refers to "that silent, darkened tropical sea" (SS 13) and the gulf that was "shadowy and silent like a phantom sea" (SS 35). Similarly, the opening narrator of *Lord Jim* refers to the "vast silence" of the ocean (LJ 50), and Jim tells Marlow repeatedly of the "silence of the sea" (*e.g.*, LJ 113, 128, 129). The commonality between non-Western space and the sea is their mutual lack of Western attributes, more particularly their lack of Western sound.

This silence of non-Western space also appears in contrast to the sound of Western space. In the Paris of *The Sisters* (1928): "Outside, the street rattled, murmured, shouted: inharmonious and busy" (S 66), while *The Arrow of Gold* (1919) opens with sound blasts of festival encompassing Marseilles: "Companies of masks with linked arms and whooping like red Indians swept the streets in crazy rushes" (AG 9), what Monsieur George calls "the bedlamite yells of carnival in the street" (AG 15). Similarly, the narrator of "Karain" points to the London Strand where he and Jackson hear the shuffle and beat of "rapid footsteps," the "vivacious" speech of passing girls, the flapping of the tails of an overcoat, the sound of hansoms, horses, and passing omnibuses, men "discussing," and an old man yelling "horribly" (K 48-49). Most dramatically, *The Secret Agent* (1907), set entirely in London, strongly connects Western space with sound: "The murmur of town life, the subdued rumble of wheels in the two invisible streets to the right and left, came through the curve of the sordid lane to [Chief Inspector Heat's] ears with a precious familiarity and an appealing sweetness" (SA 103). An even more pronounced instance arises during the journey from Mr. Verloc's shop to the charity home. Throughout this scene, the singularly dominant sensory impression is the sound of the space they traverse: "In the narrow streets the progress of the journey was made sensible to those within by the near fronts of the houses gliding past slowly and shakily, with a great rattle and jingling of glass, as if about to collapse behind the cab" (SA 147). In the cab, Winnie and her mother experience "the jolting, rattling, and jingling of the journey" and must go so far as to scream "above the noise" to hear one another (SA 148). Far from the silence of the African expanse or Malay wilderness or open ocean, the streets of the West project sound in the absence of silence, and throughout, sound is a dominant element of these Western settings.

An even clearer comparison between Western and non-Western space emerges in those works that directly contrast how sound and silence associate with spatial distinctions. By implication, this distinction emerges early in *Heart of Darkness* where Marlow associates Western space with action and sound. He chronicles his rushing round London as he prepares to leave for his interview on the continent (HD 55), and once he arrives in the "sepulchral city," he points out that voices everywhere speak enthusiastically of the trading company (HD 59). In reality, Marlow reserves silence in Western space solely for the trading company itself, which he consistently describes in the same terms of silence he later does African space, identifying, for instance, the "dead silence" (HD 59) surrounding the company building and characterizing it as being "as still as a house in a city of the dead" (HD 61). In so doing, Marlow incontrovertibly connects the company to African space[8] (something that becomes increasingly apparent as the story progresses), and in this moment Marlow the narrator first points toward a conflation of Western and African space, a place where Marlow the character will arrive at the conclusion to his journey.

In *Heart of Darkness*, the distinction between the sound of Europe and the silence of Africa is implied rather than voiced and occurs when Marlow describes each space as he encounters it. Similar to but also different from *Heart of Darkness*, *"Narcissus"* describes sound-filled and sound-absent spaces separately, but rather than how Marlow travels from sound to silence and back to sound in going from Europe to Africa and then back to Europe, the space of the ship in effect changes depending on where it is located. At sea, the *Narcissus* is enveloped in silence (except during the storm),[9] and this effect is particularly prominent with the silent and still doldrums that the ship suffers during James Wait's final illness. Once his body leaves the ship, the calms cease, and within a paragraph the narrative has leaped ahead a week in chronology to the *Narcissus* entering the English Channel. The effect is that the ship rests in a space of silence and then suddenly enters a space of sound when it proceeds up the Thames River amidst an ever-increasing amplitude of sound, edging ever closer to London, to what many saw as the epicenter of the Western world. Once the ship reaches port, it is engulfed in sound, engulfed in the "roar of the town" (NN 254):

[8] Even the company itself enjoins Marlow to equate it with silence when it requires him to undertake "amongst other things not to disclose any trade secrets" (HD 60).

[9] There is of course a great deal of sound during the storm, but the noise of the storm functions more like silence than sound since it is a white noise that actually extinguishes the sound of the sailors' voices whenever they try to communicate with one another (*e.g.*, NN 180). The storm in *Typhoon* (1902) evokes an analogous effect (*e.g.*, Ty 282-83), and in "The Black Mate," "Even in gales of wind everything went on quietly somehow" (BM 97).

> Long drifts of smoky vapours soiled it [the *Narcissus*] with livid trails; it [London] throbbed to the beat of millions of hearts, and from it came an immense and lamentable murmur – the murmur of millions of lips praying, cursing, sighing, jeering – the undying murmur of folly, regret, and hope exhaled by the crowds of the anxious earth. The *Narcissus* entered the cloud; the shadows deepened; on all sides there was the clang of iron, the sound of mighty blows, shrieks, yells. … A mad jumble of begrimed walls loomed up vaguely in the smoke, bewildering and mournful, like a vision of disaster. (NN 248)

Contrary to the silence and solitude of the sea, London teems with sound and activity and stands in strict distinction to the silence of the sea, the imprint made greater by the almost direct comparison effected when the narrative skips a week's sailing to arrive at a space submerged in sound. This impression repeats multiple times as the *Narcissus* approaches its final destination:

> One of the women screamed at the silent ship – "Hallo, Jack!" without looking at any one in particular, and all hands looked at her from the forecastle head. – "Stand clear! Stand clear of that rope!" cried the dockmen, bending over stone posts. The crowd murmured, stamped where they stood. – "Let go your quarter-checks! Let go!" sang out a ruddy-faced old man on the quay. The ropes splashed heavily falling in the water, and the *Narcissus* entered the dock. (NN 248-49)

The sound and activity of the Western world extinguish the silence and solitude of the sea, as the woman screams at "the silent ship," and the spatial silence of a week prior has become a flickering remembrance, extinguished by the sound of the city, as London assimilates the *Narcissus* and transforms the ship into a space of sound.

Making this contrast between Western sound and non-Western silence even more dramatic, "Karain" establishes a particularly powerful contrast between the silence of the non-Western world and the sound of the Western world. When Karain finishes his tale of ghostly haunting, the narrator remarks, "The silence was profound; but it seemed full of noiseless phantoms, of things sorrowful, shadowy, and mute." In response to this silence, in response to its "invisible presence," the Western sound of "the firm, pulsating beat of the two ship's chronometers ticking off steadily the seconds of Greenwich Time" seemed to the narrator to be "a protection and a relief" (K 38) that muffles the surrounding silence. Karain's tale temporarily transforms the space of the ship (an enclave of the West in this non-Western world) into a space overwhelmed by the silence of the non-West. The sound of the chronometers, however, emblems of Western science and purveyors of Western sound, restore the ship to its state of Western space and sound.

Late in the story, as noted earlier, an even more pronounced effect occurs during a chance encounter on the streets of London when the narrator tries to convince Jackson concerning the unreality of Karain's world and the reality of the Western world: "My dear chap, you have been too long away from home. What a question to ask! Only look at all this," pointing to the street:

> Our ears were filled by a headlong shuffle and beat of rapid footsteps and by an underlying rumour – a rumour vast, faint, pulsating, as of panting breaths, of beating hearts, of gasping voices; ... two young girls passed by, talking vivaciously and with shining eyes; ... a knot of dirty men with red neckerchiefs round their bare throats lurched along, discussing filthily; a ragged old man with a face of despair yelled horribly in the mud the name of a paper. (K 48-49)

Cedric Watts remarks that the narrator "thus invokes the city, implying that all around them is a solid guarantee of familiar realities. So, in response to a questioner who is tempted by the 'absurd' notion that a real ghost might have been exorcised by a charm, the narrator seeks to exorcise this regression into superstition by invoking everyday urban reality" (22), but the narrator also suggests that the activity and sound of London, provide a reality and meaning that the stillness and silence of Karain's land does not, in the same way that in *"Narcissus"* the sound of London cancels the silence of the sea.

A judicial juxtaposition of sound and silence, side by side, occurs as well at the close of "An Outpost of Progress" when the narrator brings together Western sound and non-Western silence. While Kayerts awakes to a "mist penetrating, enveloping and silent," he suddenly hears

> [a] shriek inhuman, vibrating and sudden, pierced like a sharp dart the white shroud of that land of sorrow. Three short, impatient screeches followed – and then, for a time, the fog-wreathes rolled on undisturbed, through a formidable silence. Then many more shrieks, rapid and piercing, like the yells of some exasperated and ruthless creature, rent the air. (OP 98)

These shrieks of the steamboat whistle announce its arrival at the outpost and erect a contrast with the silence of African space, entirely drowning it out.

"Youth" also opposes the sound of the West with the silence of the non-West. As referenced previously, when Marlow approaches the Eastern shore for the first time, he finds a space enveloped in silence, one he equates with silence (Y38-39). As he reaches the dock, though, he recalls: "And then, before I could open my lips, the East spoke to me, but it was in a Western voice. A torrent of words was poured into the enigmatical, the fateful silence; outlandish, angry words. … The voice swore and cursed violently; it riddled the solemn peace of the bay by a volley of abuse" (Y 40). The silent scene Marlow had just beheld is overwhelmed by the sound of the Western voice. This effect is exacerbated by the contrast between the crass abuse contained in the Western sound alongside the mystical enchantment ensconced in the Eastern silence.

Despite the seeming stark distinction between Western sound and non-Western silence, where sound seems to subdue silence, the dichotomy in truth breaks down. This effect is only implied in "An Outpost of Progress." Nevertheless, despite the sudden appearance of steamer's screeching whistle that extinguishes the pervasive silence that Kayerts experiences just before its arrival, we know that when the steamboat departs after the conclusion to the story that the silence of Africa will return to replace the sound of the West. In *The Rescue*, this effect becomes actual: on the Western space of the ship, the night-watchman's "footsteps died out forward, and a somnolent, unbreathing repose took possession of the stranded yacht" (R 150). As the sound of the watchman's passing disappears into the darkness, the silence of Eastern space flows into the sonic void left in the wake of Western footsteps. In the same way, in *The Shadow-Line*, after the captain and Ransome converse, "the profound silence [of the sea] returned" (SL 108). Again, Western sound only momentarily displaces non-Western silence. Even more dramatically, in "Youth," once the "Western voice" (Y 40) ceases cursing "the silence was as complete as though it had never been broken" (Y 41). In spite of the sound of this Western voice, silence remains the dominant feature of this Eastern space. Each incident demonstrates the play between the sound of the Western world and the silence of the non-Western world.

In *"Narcissus,"* silence does not replace the sound of the West, as it does in "An Outpost of Progress," "Youth," and *The Rescue*. In fact, as suggested above, the sound of London entirely engulfs the silence of the open ocean. Nevertheless, the silence of the sea remains prominent in the mind of the reader and in the memory of the men of the *Narcissus* as Conrad presents the crew as weak and aimless once removed from the silent ocean. This effect appears most prominently in Singleton, who becomes a doddering old man on land in contrast to his stately majesty at sea. Furthermore, Conrad clearly affirms those he associates with the silence of the sea as opposed to those he associates with the sound of the land: Donkin, who will hereafter "'ave a job hashore" (NN 252) and the pay clerk who sees Singleton as "a disgusting old brute" (NN 251). Both men stand sharply contrasted against the men of the silent seas. In a metaphorical manner, the silence of the sea, like the silence of the East in "Youth," has flowed back into the space the men inhabit, as the silence of the sea remains with the characters' (and reader's) memories even amidst the sounds of London. And despite the narrator of "Karain"'s confidence in the sound of the West, Jackson is less convinced, replying: "Yes; I see it. It is there; it pants, it runs, it rolls; it is strong and alive; it would smash you if you didn't look out; but I'll be hanged if it is yet as real to me as … as the other thing … say, Karain's story" (K 49). Jackson acknowledges the power of the sound of London, but it cannot obliterate his memory of the still silence surrounding Karain's tale. As a result, in the midst of London, Karain's land maintains a poignant place in Jackson's mind.

Several incidents in *Heart of Darkness*, similarly contrast Western sound with non-Western silence: "We stopped, and the silence driven away by the stamping of our feet flowed back again from the recesses of the land" (HD 86); "The word ivory would ring in the air for a while – and on we went again into the silence" (HD 93); "a few dropping shots rang out sharply – then silence" (HD 107). An even more graphic incident occurs shortly after Marlow first arrives at the company's outer station when he encounters what he calls "objectless blasting": "A heavy and dull detonation shoot the ground, a puff of smoke came out of the cliff, and that was all. No change appeared on the face of the rock" (HD 67). In this instance, not only is there no permanent sonic effect, with silence replacing sound after each blast, but the unchanged cliff serves as a metaphor for the ineffectual sound. Neither the sound nor the blast has any permanent impact on the silent surrounding space. Western sound temporarily displaces non-Western silence – but only to see silence return and replace sound, sound having no more result than a pebble dropped in a pond, which momentarily displaces the water only to see that displacement dissipate as the water flows back to its previous position. In each incident, Western sound displaces non-Western silence – but the effect is transitory, as non-Western silence flows back to extinguish Western sound.

This effect appears most strikingly in *The End of the Tether*: "The thump of the engines reverberated regularly like the strokes of a metronome beating the measure of the vast silence" (ET 229). Here the narrator experiences not a displacement of one for the other but rather a conjoining of Western sound and non-Western silence, as the sound of the engine measures out not sound but silence. This relationship between Western sound and non-Western silence is an early portent of a more pervasive phenomenon that will gradually grow and gradually divulge the distinctions between West and non-West to be superficial rather than substantive. Before arriving at that conclusion, however, Conrad's characters must endure the important implications of the silence of non-Western space, when Conrad's narrators associate the absence of sound with a more general absence and consistently describe silence space also as empty space.

In "An Outpost of Progress," for example, the traders perceive the Congo as "very empty" (OP 92), a "great emptiness" (OP 81), and a "void" (OP 81), while in *Heart of Darkness*, it is "empty" (HD 73), an "empty immensity" (HD 65), and an "empty land" (HD 73), containing an "empty stream" (HD 91) with "empty reaches" (HD 93). Kayerts, Carlier, and Marlow experience Africa as both silent and empty. In *Lord Jim*, the silent space surrounding the *Patna*'s lifeboat is such that one "couldn't distinguish the sea from the sky; there was nothing to see and nothing to hear. Not a glimmer, not a shape, not a sound. You could have believed that every bit of dry land had gone to the bottom" (LJ 128). All objects have disappeared, leaving only empty space in their place. Later, Marlow describes Patusan as an "empty space" (LJ 338), containing a river of "empty reaches" (LJ 234, 301, 326). In this same way, Arsat's land in "The Lagoon" is one of "empty distances" (L 166) surrounded by "the empty and broad expanse of the sea-reach" (L 155), while Lena experiences the "empty space" of the East, which was to her "the abomination of desolation" (V 156). Almayer's silent Sambir is similar:

> There was not a glimmer of light in the sky now, and the tops of the trees were as invisible as their trunks, being lost in the mass of clouds that hung low over the woods, the clearing, and the river. Every outline had disappeared in the intense blackness that seemed to have destroyed everything but space. Only the fire glimmered like a star forgotten in this annihilation of all visible things. (AF 143)

More dramatic, the space of the East is a "black void" (AF 115), as is Karain's land, which for the narrator is "still, complete, unknown," containing an "empty beach" (K 13, 24) and an "empty river" (K 31), amidst villages that appear "deserted" (K 24), a land that "seemed unaccountably empty of anything that would stir the thought, touch the heart, give a hint of the ominous sequence of days" (K 14). Analogous Eastern space exists as well in *The Rescue*:

> The coast off which the little brig, floating upright above her anchor, seemed to guard the high hull of the yacht has no distinctive features. It is land without form. It stretches away without cape or bluff, long and low – indefinitely; and when the heavy gusts of the northeast monsoon drive the thick rain slanting over the sea, it is seen faintly under the grey sky, black and with a blurred outline like the straight edge of a dissolving shore. (R 63)

More explicitly, Mrs. Travers remarks of this space, "How quiet it is! … How unnaturally quiet! It is like a desert of land and water without a living soul" (R 149), and the narrator suggests, "Not a sound broke the stillness and she felt as if she were lost in empty space" (R 167). Finally, the narrator of "The Warrior's Soul" (1917) refers to the silent Russian expanses as "empty spaces" (WS 1). Consistently, the same space the characters experience as silent they also experience as empty.

The sea is similar, the same silent sea of *Almayer's Folly*, *"Narcissus,"* *Lord Jim* and *Victory*, for example, is also "empty" (AF 154, NN 223, LJ 171, and V 34 respectively), and on a "barren" sea, the captain in *The Shadow-Line* "faced an empty world, steeped in an infinity of silence" (SL 107). In *"Narcissus,"* the sea is an "abyss" (NN 161). In *The Rescue*, it is a "clear blue abyss" (R 285), and in *Victory* it is a "flaming abyss of emptiness" (V 169). In this same way, *The End of the Tether* discloses "the spacious silence of the empty sea" (ET 198), where the *Sofala* travels "smoothly in the somber void" (ET 217; see also 206 and 280). More even than the emptiness of Africa, the East and elsewhere in the non-Western world, which is of course a metaphorical emptiness, the sea graphically reveals a literal emptiness, as Conrad's characters on the open ocean experience the absence of all objects but themselves, their ship, and the undemarcated ocean itself.

In all of these stories, the sonic absence of space is a metonym for a larger absence: the absence of familiar geography, order, values, and meaning. In "Youth," Marlow relates: "I had faced the silence of the East. I had heard some of its languages" (Y 41), but even after having heard the language of the East (which he only perceived as incomprehensible sound), Marlow continues to correlate the East with silence to the end of the story. Regardless of any sound Marlow may encounter in the East, its dominant state is not sound but silence because its sound is not Western sound.[10] "An Outpost of Progress" elaborates: for Kayerts and Carlier the silence of Africa is the absence of sound, but it is also the absence of what they perceive to be meaningful sound, and the emptiness of Africa is the absence of activity (stillness) but also the absence of what they perceive to be meaningful activity: "The river, the forest, all the great land throbbing with life, were like a great emptiness. Even the brilliant sunshine disclosed nothing intelligible. Things appeared and disappeared before their eyes in an unconnected and aimless kind of way. The river seemed to come from nowhere and flow nowhither. It flowed through a void" (OP 81). Kayerts and Carlier see a "great land throbbing with life" that they perceive at the same time as "a great emptiness," containing a river that "seemed to come from nowhere and flow nowhither ... through a void," a void that "disclosed nothing intelligible" (OP 81). Similarly, they hear "sudden yells that resembled snatches of songs from a madhouse [that] darted shrill and high in discordant jets of sound" (OP 86). Annika J. Lindskog rightly recognizes this same effect in *Heart of Darkness*, contending that "what the jungle lacks are the sounds of civilization" (47-48).[11] For instance, Marlow recounts that as the steamboat "struggled round a bend, there would be a glimpse of rush walls, of peaked grass-roofs, a burst of yells, a whirl of black limbs, a mass of hands clapping, of feet stamping, of bodies swaying, of eyes rolling, under the droop of heavy and motionless foliage. The steamer toiled along slowly on the edge of a black and incomprehensible frenzy" (HD 93). Marlow wonders whether "prehistoric man was

[10] The first three chapters of Robert Hampson's *Cross-Cultural Encounters in Joseph Conrad's Malay Fiction* chronicles how from William Marsden, Thomas Stamford Raffles, and James Brooke to Alfred Russel Wallace and Hugh Clifford Westerners constructed a perception of the Malay world rather than a representation of it. Hampson's argument has some affinities with mine, although I focus on the absence that Conrad's characters project onto the non-Western world.

[11] Sarah Dauncey suggests something similar concerning Conrad's vision in *Victory*: "Instead of seeing the island's quietness as a product of Conrad's Eurocentric outlook which is unable to conceive of the indigenous peoples of colonial worlds as active and historical subjects, it must be understood in the light of the novel's acts of silent, strategic, resistance" (152).

cursing us, praying to us, welcoming us – who could tell?" because the Westerners were "cut off from [their] surroundings; [they] glided past like phantoms, wondering and secretly appalled, as sane men would be before an enthusiastic outbreak in a madhouse" (HD 93-94). Sound is engulfed by even more pervasive silence because, like Kayerts and Carlier, the sound has no meaning for Marlow ("who could tell?"). In these tales, non-Western space appears only as a silent and still emptiness because its sound and activity are not Western sound and activity and therefore lack the meaning the Westerners assign to them. At the same time, though, this absence will later cause Conrad's characters to reconsider the meaning they assign to Western sound and activity. As they experience this bond between silent space and empty space, they also begin the process toward the darkening enlightenment of absence.

References

Achebe, Chinua. "An Image of Africa." *Massachusetts Review*, vol. 18, no. 4, winter 1977, pp. 782–94.

Baxter, Katherine Isobel. "The Strange Spaces of *The Rescue*." *The Conradian*, vol. 29, no. 1, spring 2004, pp. 64–83.

Casarino, Cesare. *Modernity at Sea: Melville, Marx, Conrad in Crisis*. Minneapolis: University of Minnesota Press, 2002, pp. 184–244.

Conrad, Joseph. *Almayer's Folly*. Edited by Peter Lancelot Mallios. New York: Modern Library, 2002.

———. *The Arrow of Gold*. Uniform edition. Garden City, NY: Doubleday, Page, 1925.

———. "Author's Note to *Tales of Unrest*." *Tales of Unrest*. Edited by Allan H. Simmons and J. H. Stape. Cambridge: Cambridge University Press, 2012, pp. 5–8.

———. "Author's Note to *Youth: A Narrative and Two Other Stories*." *Heart of Darkness*. Edited by John G. Peters. Peterborough, Ontario: Broadview Press, 2019, pp. 45–47.

———. "Because of the Dollars." *Within the Tides*. Edited by Alexandre, Laurence Davies, and Andrew Purssell. Cambridge: Cambridge University Press, 2012, pp. 137–68.

———. "The Black Mate." *Tales of Hearsay*. Uniform edition. Garden City, NY: Doubleday, Page, 1925, pp. 85–120.

———. *The Collected Letters of Joseph Conrad*. Edited by Laurence Davies, *et al*, 9 vols. Cambridge: Cambridge University Press, 1983–2008.

———. "The Crime of Partition." *Notes on Life and Letters*. Edited by J. H. Stape. Cambridge: Cambridge: Cambridge University Press, 2004, pp. 94–107.

———. *The End of the Tether. Youth, Heart of Darkness, The End of the Tether*. Edited by John Lyon. London: Penguin, 1995, pp. 151–299.

———. "Author's Note to *Youth: A Narrative*". *Heart of Darkness*. Edited by John G. Peters. Peterborough, Ontario: Broadview Press, 2019, pp. 45-47.

———. *Heart of Darkness*. Edited by John G. Peters. Peterborough, Ontario: Broadview Press, 2019.

———. "Karain: A Memory." *Tales of Unrest*. Edited by Allan H. Simmons and J. H. Stape. Cambridge: Cambridge University Press, 2012, pp. 13–49.

———. "The Lagoon." *Tales of Unrest*. Edited by Allan H. Simmons and J. H. Stape, Cambridge University Press, 2012, pp. 155–67.

———. *Lord Jim*. Edited by Cedric Watts. Peterborough, Ontario: Broadview Press, 2001.

———. *The Nigger of the "Narcissus." The Secret Sharer and Other Stories*. Edited by John G. Peters. New York: W. W. Norton, 2015, pp. 137–254.

———. "An Outpost of Progress." *Tales of Unrest*. Edited by Allan H. Simmons and J. H. Stape. Cambridge: Cambridge University Press, 2012, pp. 77–99.

———. *A Personal Record*. Edited by Zdzisław Najder and J. H. Stape. Cambridge: Cambridge University Press, 2008.

———. *The Rescue*. Uniform edition. Garden City, NY: Doubleday, Page, 1925.

———. *The Secret Agent*. Edited by Tanya Agathocleous. Peterborough, Ontario: Broadview Press, 2009.

———. "The Secret Sharer." *The Secret Sharer and Other Stories*. Edited by John G. Peters. New York: W. W. Norton, 2015, pp. 7–42.

———. *The Shadow-Line. The Secret Sharer and Other Stories*. Edited by John G. Peters. New York: W. W. Norton, 2015, pp. 47–135.

———. *The Sisters: An Unfinished Story*. Edited by Ugo Mursia. Milan: U. Mursia & Co., 1968.

———. *Typhoon. The Secret Sharer and Other Stories*. Edited by John G. Peters. New York: W. W. Norton, 2015, pp. 259–324.

———. *Victory*. Edited by Peter Lancelot Mallios. Modern Library, 2003.

———. "The Warrior's Soul." *Tales of Hearsay*. Uniform edition. Garden City, NY: Doubleday, Page, 1925, pp. 1–26.

———. "Youth: A Narrative." *Youth, Heart of Darkness, The End of the Tether*. Edited by John Lyon. London: Penguin, 1995, pp. 9–43.

Coroneos, Con. *Space, Conrad, and Modernity*. Oxford: Oxford University Press, 2002.

Dauncey, Sarah. "'The islands are very quiet': Space and Silence in Conrad's *Victory*." *Conradiana*, vol. 42, no. 1–2, spring-summer 2010, pp. 141–54.
Fogel, Aaron. *Coercion to Speak: Conrad's Poetics of Dialogue*. Cambridge, MA: Harvard University Press, 1985.
Garnett, Edward. "Introduction." *Letters from Joseph Conrad: 1895–1924*. Edited by Edward Garnett. Indianapolis: Bobbs-Merrill, 1928, pp. 1–28.
Graver, Lawrence. *Conrad's Short Fiction*. Berkeley: University of California Press, 1969.
Hampson, Robert. *Cross-Cultural Encounters in Joseph Conrad's Malay Fiction*. New York: Palgrave, 2000.
———. "Spatial Stories: Joseph Conrad and James Joyce." *Geographies of Modernism: Literatures, Cultures, Spaces*. Edited by Peter Brooker and Andrew Thacker. London: Routledge, 2005, pp. 55–64.
Hannah, Daniel. "'Under a cloud': Silence, Identity, and Interpretation in *Lord Jim*." *Conradiana*, vol. 40, no. 1, spring 2008, pp. 39–59.
Hollahan, Eugene. "Beguiled into Action: Silence and Sound in *Victory*." *Texas Studies in Literature and Language*, vol. 6, no. 2, summer 1974, pp. 349–62.
Hooper, Myrtle J. "The Heart of Light: Silence in Conrad's *Heart of Darkness*." *Conradiana*, vol 25, no. 1, 1993, pp. 69–76.
Janechek, Jennifer A. "The Horror of the Primal Sound: Proto-telephony and Imperialism in 'Heart of Darkness.'" *The Conradian*, vol. 41, no 2, autumn 2016, pp. 8–27.
Jean-Aubry, G. *Joseph Conrad: Life and Letters*, 2 vols. Garden City, NY: Doubleday, Page, 1927.
Kort, Wesley A. *Place and Space in Modern Fiction*. Gainesville: University Press of Florida, 2004.
Krishnan, Sanjay. "Seeing the Animal: Colonial Space and Movement in Joseph Conrad's *Lord Jim*." *Novel*, vol. 37, no. 3, summer 2004, pp. 326–51.
Kurowska, Joanna. "Counter-Images of Europe in the Utterances of Selected Characters in Conrad's African Fiction." *Conrad's Europe: Conference Proceedings*. Edited by Andrzej Ciuk and Marcin Piechota. Opole, Poland: Opole University, 2005, pp. 163–70.
Lange, Attie de. "'Reading' and 'Constructing' Space, Gender and Race: Joseph Conrad's *Lord Jim* and J. M. Coetzee's *Foe*." *Literary Landscapes: From Modernism to Postcolonialism*. Edited by Attie de Lange et al. New York: Palgrave Macmillan, 2008, pp. 109–124.
Lindskog, Annika J. "'It was very quiet': The Contaminating Soundscapes of 'Heart of Darkness.'" *The Conradian*, vol. 39, no. 2, autumn 2014, pp. 44–60.
Martinière, Nathalie. "Symbolic Space and Narrative Focus: The Cabin in Conrad's Sea Stories." *The Conradian*, vol. 27, no. 1, spring 2002, pp. 24–38.

McClintock, Anne. "'Unspeakable secrets': The Ideology of Landscape in Conrad's *Heart of Darkness*." *Journal of the Midwest Modern Language Association*, vol. 17, no. 1, spring 1984, pp. 38–53.

McLeod, Deborah. "Disturbing the Silence: Sound Imagery in Conrad's *The Secret Agent*." *Journal of Modern Literature*, vol. 33, no. 1, fall 2009, pp. 117–31.

Melnick, Daniel C. "*Under Western Eyes* and Silence." *Slavic and East European Journal*, vol. 45, no. 2 summer 2001, pp. 231–42.

Mongia, Padmini. "Empire, Narrative and the Feminine in *Lord Jim* and *Heart of Darkness*." *Contexts for Conrad*. Edited by Keith Carabine, Owen Knowles, and Wiesław Krajka. Boulder, CO: East European Monographs, 1993, pp. 135–50.

Mstowska, Joanna. "Inner Sea Space in Joseph Conrad's *Youth* and *The Mirror of the Sea*." *Exploring Space: Spatial Notions in Cultural, Literary and Language Studies*. Edited by Andrzej Ciuk and Katarzyna Molek-Kozakowska, Newcastle upon Tyne: Cambridge Scholars Publishing, 2010, pp. 158–65.

Pawloski, Merry W. "Conrad's Voyage In and Woolf's *The Voyage Out*: Gender and the Production of Cultural Space." *Conrad at the Millennium: Modernism, Postmodernism, Postcolonialism*. Edited by Gail Fincham, Attie de Lange, and Wiesław Krajka. Boulder: Social Science Monographs, 2001, pp. 119–37.

Pedot, Richard. "'With sealed lips': The Enigma of Rhetoric in *Lord Jim*." *L'Epoque Conradienne*, vol. 30, 2004, pp. 185–95.

Peters, John G. "Joseph Conrad and the Epistemology of Space." *Philosophy and Literature*, vol. 4, no. 1, April 2016, pp. 98–123.

Pinsker, Sanford. "Silence and the Existential Whisper: Once Again at the 'Heart of Darkness.'" *Modern Language Studies*, vol. 2, no. 2, summer 1972, pp. 53–59.

Rawson, Eric. "'A dying vibration': Sound and Silence in *Heart of Darkness*." *Orbis Litterarum*, vol. 72, no. 1, February 2017, pp 36–50.

Ray, Martin. "Language and Silence in the Novels of Joseph Conrad." *Conradiana*, vol. 16, no.1, spring 1984, pp. 19–40.

Richardson, Brian. "Silence, Progression, and Narrative Collapse in Conrad." *Conradiana*, vol. 46, no. 1–2, spring-summer 2014, pp. 109–21.

Sewlall, Harry. "Postcolonial/Postmodern Spaciality in *Almayer's Folly* and *An Outcast of the Islands*." *Conradiana*, vol. 38, no. 1, spring 2006, pp. 79–93.

Sönmez, Margaret J-M. "The Speech and Silences of Orientals in Conrad's Novels." *Joseph Conrad and the Orient*. Edited by Amar Acheraïou and Nursel Içöz. Boulder, CO: East European Monographs, 2012, pp. 263–301.

Trench-Bonett, Dorothy. "Naming and Silence: A Study of Language and the Other in Conrad's *Heart of Darkness*." *Conradiana*, vol. 32, no. 2, summer 2000, pp. 84–95.

Wasserman, Jerry. "Narrative Presence: The Illusion of Language in *Heart of Darkness*." *Studies in the Novel*, vol. 6, no. 3, fall 1974, pp. 327–38.

Watts, Cedric. "Conrad and the Myth of the Monstrous Town." *Conrad's Cities: Essays for Hans van Marle*. Edited by Gene M. Moore. Amsterdam: Rodopi, 1992, pp. 17–30.

White, Allon. *The Uses of Obscurity: The Fictions of Early Modernism*. London: Routledge & Kegan Paul, 1981.

CHAPTER 3

Western Space in Non-Western Space

Abstract This chapter considers Western spaces that exist within non-Western space: the various trading stations and similar establishments that appear in so many of Conrad's works. This chapter argues that these Western enclaves are established as havens of sound and activity in contrast to the silence and emptiness of the surrounding non-Western space. In the end, however, such spaces prove to be mere facades that either gradually lose any distinction that might have originally existed between such spaces and the surrounding non-Western space, or such distinctions have disappeared by the beginning the tale, or they have never existed in the first place. As a result, barriers break down between these enclaves of Western space and the non-Western space that surrounds them.

Keywords Joseph Conrad • Western space • Non-Western space • Ethics • Emptiness

To this point, I have considered Western space and non-Western space within their individual spheres of existence: Western space as it appears in the West and non-Western space as it appears in the non-West. But there exist in Conrad's works various enclaves of Western space outside the West, Western space that exists in fact within non-Western space, and these enclaves are meant to be metaphorical Western spaces that reflect the West.

J. G. Peters, *Silence, Space and Absence in Conrad's Works*,
https://doi.org/10.1007/978-3-031-44910-9_3

The heavily Western-influenced Eastern cities of Bangkok and Singapore of *Falk* (1903), *The Shadow-Line*, *Lord Jim*, *The End of the Tether*, and "Because of the Dollars," for instance, are such spaces, as are the trading stations of "An Outpost of Progress," *Heart of Darkness*, *Victory*, *Lord Jim*, *Almayer's Folly*, and *An Outcast of the Islands*.[1] The Westerners who establish these enclaves see a distinct difference between Western and non-Western space and seek either to transform non-Western space into Western space or to establish and maintain Western space within the confines of their enclaves (in contrast to the non-Western space around them), thereby also maintaining what Westerners perceive to be absolute differences between the West and the non-West. In both instances, the goal is to recreate Western government, customs, and values in place of those of the non-West. Invariably, though, these Western spaces within non-Western spaces lose or never establish the unbending boundaries between Western and non-Western space that their founders envision, and these boundaries between what they see as Western spaces of sound and fullness and non-Western spaces of silence and emptiness eventually blur, thus undermining Western ideas of unbridgeable barriers between the West and the non-West.

Both the non-Western cities with strong Western presences and the Western trading posts within non-Western space bear a commonality – what I term the narrative of benefit: the narrative that the Western world benefitted the non-Western world by disseminating its values. The frame narrator in *Heart of Darkness* alludes to this narrative when he muses on the history of the Thames River: "Hunters for gold or pursuers of fame, they all had gone out on that stream, bearing the sword, and often the torch, messengers of the might within the land, bearers of a spark from the sacred fire" (HD 52). The "torch" and the "spark from the sacred fire" that these "messengers" carried are metaphors for the narrative of benefit. Elsewhere, Marlow articulates this narrative even more clearly: "There were very few places in the Archipelago he [Stein] had not seen in the original dusk of their being, before light (and even electric light) had been carried into them for the sake of better morality and – and – well – the greater profit too" (LJ 212-13). The "light" Marlow references is the light of Western civilization, which was regularly represented in Western society as enlightening the darkened world of the non-West and as the sole

[1] The various vessels that traverse the Eastern seas and open ocean in Conrad's writings also exist as enclaves of Western space in the non-Western world.

reason for colonizing the non-Western world.[2] This "light" entailed disseminating Western government, customs, technology, religion, and especially morality, in short what the West perceived as "Truth." The reality that trade occurred on an enormous and exploitative scale was suppressed, subsumed by the narrative of benefit. Westerners believed their morality to be superior to what they saw as the immorality of the non-West, and they considered all enclaves of the West within the non-West as models for a moral society.[3] When Marlow talks of light being carried to the archipelago, he also hints at the actuality of the situation: that the narrative of benefit was largely an excuse to exploit, as he hesitatingly acknowledges that the dissemination of "light" was for "well – the greater profit too." Ultimately, the scarcity of benefit (for the colonized) and the abundance of profit (for the colonizers) proves to be one of the primary means that the West fails to create itself as a space superior to the non-West.

The effect of trying to establish Western enclaves in the non-West has different results in different instances. Of the major cities in Conrad's works with a powerful Western presence in the non-Western world (specifically Bangkok and Singapore), each in its own way reveals an unsuccessful attempt to establish distinctions between Western space and non-Western space. In the case of Bangkok, despite a strong Western presence, it is always a minority presence, both in population and in power. For the most part, this results from the fact that Siam, although the victim of unequal treaties with Western powers throughout the nineteenth century, nevertheless never became a Western colony, unlike so much of southeast Asia. Bangkok appears particularly prominently in *Falk* and *The Shadow-Line*, but in both works, despite its prominent place, Western

[2] Kurtz's painting ironically inverts the narrative of benefit, representing "a woman, draped and blindfolded, carrying a lighted torch. The background was sombre – almost black. The movement of the woman was stately, and the effect of the torchlight on the face was sinister" (HD 80). The woman is blindfolded and thus cannot see what she does, and her lighted torch does not illuminate the "somber – almost black" background but instead reveals not the beneficent face of a benefactor but the "sinister" one of a conqueror.

[3] It could be argued, of course, that this Western code of morality is also absent from Western space, that Westerners were hypocritical in espousing a moral code that they themselves failed to follow, particularly in relation to the non-Western world. However, the fact that this system of morality is touted as an element of Western space is what is important here, not necessarily whether Westerners practiced their espoused values. Furthermore, that Westerners were routinely guilty of the very lack of morality of which they accused the non-Western world serves to remove rather than reinforce Western perceived partitions between Western and non-Western space.

space never gains a strong standing. *The Shadow-Line* best demonstrates this phenomenon by way of contrast with Singapore (which also appears in the novel). When comparing the Western presence in both cities, we clearly see a lesser presence in Bangkok. "Youth" underscores this reality. Marlow remarks that he "wanted awfully to get to Bankok [*sic*]. To Bankok! Magic name, blessed name. Mesopotamia wasn't a patch on it" (Y 19). For the young Marlow, Bangkok holds only the exoticism he imagines of the East, not reflections of the West, and this effect is evident in other works where Bangkok appears prominently. Overall, distinctions between Eastern and Western space never wholly take hold in Bangkok, and Eastern and Western spaces there are largely indistinguishable.

Singapore is different. Particularly because it was a colony. From the outset of its many appearances in Conrad's writings, its state differs from Bangkok's. Singapore was the seat of the British empire in the Malay Archipelago, and whenever it appears in Conrad's writings, it is dominated by elements of the West. From the central government offices to the central shipping offices to its Western establishments, such as the Officers' Sailors' Home in *The Shadow-Line*, Singapore appears almost to be a Western city. Unlike Bangkok, where spatial distinctions between East and West dissolve because they are never really realized, Singapore's Eastern and Western boundaries blur because, despite the power of Western pressure, the Westerners remain a great minority. They have political but not populous power. This prevents the metaphorical erection of boundaries between Eastern and Western space, and regardless of how they may try to transform this Eastern space into Western space, the two remain indivisible from one another.[4]

The boundaries between Western and non-Western space that those establishing Conrad's trading posts seek to erect, though, dissolve differently from those in Bangkok and Singapore. They also dissolve differently from one another, but they nonetheless exhibit common features. In each enclave, the physical degeneration that transpires mirrors the metaphorical degeneration of the boundaries between the Western space within these stations and the non-Western space outside them. Sometimes this physical degeneration has happened prior to the opening of the tale (*e.g.*, *Almayer's Folly*, *Heart of Darkness*, *Victory*, and *Lord Jim*); sometimes it happens during the tale (*e.g.*, "An Outpost of Progress" and *An Outcast of the*

[4] Singapore's eventual political independence underscores the fact that it never became a wholly Western space.

Islands). Moreover, the degeneration of espoused Western morality and values within the stations metaphorically mirrors the physical degeneration that evolved in these Western spaces. Given the prominent position of Western ethical values in the narrative of benefit, their complete lack or gradual disappearance effectively extinguishes boundaries between the Western and the non-Western in these spaces, such that these stations eventually no longer exhibit Western values and hence are no longer Western spaces.[5]

Among the trading posts appearing in Conrad's works, Stein's Patusan station is the least autonomous and most remote. The novel makes clear that few have even heard of Patusan (LJ 212); none (except Stein and Cornelius) have ever been there, and Marlow likens Jim's going there to being sent to "a star of the fifth magnitude" because "the change could not have been greater" (LJ 212). Such an enormous difference between the fledgling Western space of the station and the ancient Eastern space of Patusan almost entirely overwhelms the trading station. The very fact, though, that the station was established with a Western presence initially sets it apart from the surrounding non-Western space, but by the time the trading post is first mentioned, its boundaries between Western and non-Western space have already disappeared. Trade (its primary purpose for being) has long since ceased, as has communication with the outside world (some thirteen months since Stein had heard any news, LJ 220). Cornelius, the station's Western presence, has appropriated whatever remaining goods Stein had sent him, and he sends no trade out of Patusan. With no goods to trade with and no goods traded for, this space is a trading station only by designation. Cornelius also assimilates himself into the local community, including marrying Jewel's mother, a local woman. Further telling, even after Jewel's mother dies and Jim replaces him as Stein's agent, Cornelius chooses to remain in Patusan.

Local politics add to the assimilation of the station into Eastern space. The trading post exists among Tunku Allang's followers, Doramin's followers, and Sherif Ali's followers, who represent the three points of power in Patusan. These political powers dominate Cornelius's station, and, unlike other enclaves of Western influence in non-Western space, under

[5] Although the narrative of benefit generally posited an absence of ethics among non-Western populations, this accusation was, of course, false. Like all societies, indigenous societies have strict ethical codes, but because these codes often differed from Western ethical codes, Westerners projected an absence of ethical codes onto non-Western cultures.

Cornelius, the station exerts no political influence over the region. Under Jim's direction, the trading post begins to establish greater autonomy and resemblance to Western space. He clears the ground around the station with the idea of creating a coffee plantation (LJ 294), and his influence on local politics is profound. Jim leads the forces that rout Sherif Ali and drive him from the land, and although he pays respect to Tunku Allang, the Rajah is terrified of Jim's influence (LJ 239). Doramin is the region's primary ruler once Jim helps expel Ali, but they appear to be nearly co-rulers, so great is Jim's standing among the local population. Despite Jim's prominence and the difference between the state of Stein's trading post under Jim's direction compared to its state under Cornelius, the distinctions between the Western space of the station and the surrounding Eastern space break down on a number of levels.

While in other Western spaces within non-Western space clear cut demarcations exist between Westerners and non-Westerners (borne out of Western convictions of their superiority to non-Westerners), these distinctions are largely non-existent in Patusan. Jim, while holding a powerful political place, nevertheless defers to Doramin as having the final word in ruling the region. He also takes Jewel, a local woman, not as a mere mistress but as his common-law wife. His best friend is Dain Waris, Doramin's son, and he speaks of the local people as "his people" (LJ 303, 342), less in the patronizing manner of typical colonial rulers than as Western rulers might refer to their subjects. The inviolable racial boundaries of the typical Western enclave in the non-Western world are almost entirely absent from Patusan.

Furthermore, although Jim maintains his Western value system, none of those around him either understand or accept those values. Jewel and Dain Waris, for example, advocate for an entirely different approach to ridding the region of Brown's men, an approach at odds with Jim's Western code of behavior (LJ 345). Similarly, neither Jewel nor Tamb' Itam concurs with, nor understands, Jim's behavior after the disaster at Dain Waris's outpost. In other words, Jim is entirely unsuccessful at disseminating Western values to the local population, the most touted tenet of the narrative of benefit. Most telling, though, all traces of the West disappear with Jim's death. There remains no Western influence on local affairs, and it seems clear from the close of the novel that the trading station has been abandoned. In effect, any remnant of the West has vanished from the land, along with what few demarcations existed to discriminate Western from non-Western space.

The conflict between ethical values at the station contributes to the breakdown of boundaries between Eastern and Western space. The ethical code of the narrative of benefit would abhor, for example, Sherif Ali's view that "Jim was to be murdered mainly on religious grounds, ... A simple act of piety (and so far infinitely meritorious)" (LJ 286), as well as Tunku Allang's machinations to bring about Jim's downfall (LJ 332-33). In the end, though, it is a Westerner who effectually accomplishes the task. The immorality of Gentleman Brown and his men could never be confused with the ethics espoused by the narrative of benefit. Nevertheless, we see the extreme immorality of Brown on display in and around this ostensible enclave of Western space. Jim's ethical values reflect those of the narrative of benefit, but his ethics cannot withstand the assault of Brown's lack of ethics, and the most powerful ethical presence at the station is Brown's absence of Western ethics, thereby revealing Western morality to be merely a social contract, which dissolves when Brown, a Westerner, refuses to abide by this contract. The overwhelming influence of Brown's immorality subsumes the ethical values espoused by the West, and their defeat metaphorically mirrors the physical signs of dissolving distinctions between Eastern and Western space in Patusan. At the novel's close, all Western presence has disappeared from Patusan, and Stein's station, originally intended to be distinct from its non-Western surroundings, has become an indistinguishable part of the silent, empty space of Patusan.

The most unusual of these enclaves of Western space is the station in *Victory*. In fact, it is something of a misnomer to refer to the defunct Tropical Coal Belt Company station as a station at all, first because it is a mining operation rather than a trading post and second because it is entirely defunct when the novel opens. Still, as an enclave of Western space, it functions in several ways similarly to the true trading posts of "An Outpost of Progress," *Heart of Darkness*, *Lord Jim*, *Almayer's Folly*, and *An Outcast of the Islands*, for instance. As an island outpost, the natural geographical boundaries reflect metaphorical boundaries between the Western space of the station on Samburan and the Eastern space of the surrounding islands of the archipelago. Furthermore, although the station is a mining facility, its separation from surrounding space reflects the typical boundaries erected between Western and non-Western spaces at other trading posts. In some ways, Samburan's Tropical Coal Belt Company station is even more isolated. Although Samburan is not uninhabited when Tropical Coal Belt Company establishes their station there, the local Alfuro people, fearing the influx of Westerners, "had blocked the path over the ridge by felling a few trees, and had kept strictly on their own side" (V 140). This boundary clearly delineates the Western space of the station from the non-Western space of the Alfuro community, and this boundary is strictly maintained, only disappearing after the death of Heyst and the erasure of the last remnants of the company. At that point, no distinctions exist between Western and Eastern space. During the short time that the company flourishes, clear demarcations exhibit themselves between Eastern and Western space, and the station mirrors Heyst's own variation on the narrative of benefit in his philosophy of "stride forward" (V 5), which embodies the ideas of progress and improvement that are so valued in the narrative of benefit.

The most obvious way the metaphorical boundaries between Eastern and Western space disappear in Samburan is with the bankruptcy of the Tropical Coal Belt Company. Early on, the narrator relates, "Heyst could see his immediate surroundings, which had the aspect of an abandoned settlement invaded by the jungle: vague roofs above low vegetation, broken shadows of bamboo fences in the sheen of long grass, something like an overgrown bit of road slanting among ragged thickets towards the shore only a couple of hundred yards away" (4). However, "the most conspicuous object was a gigantic blackboard raised on two posts and presenting to Heyst, when the moon got over that side, the white letters 'T. B. C. Co.' in a row at least two feet high" (V 4-5). Later, the narrator elaborates on the state of the station:

> That black jetty, sticking out of the jungle into the empty sea; these roof-ridges of deserted houses peeping dismally above the long grass! Ough! The gigantic and funereal blackboard sign of the Tropical Belt Coal Company, still emerging from a wild growth of bushes like an inscription stuck above a grave figured by the tall heap of unsold coal at the shore end of the wharf, added to the general desolation. (V 34-35)

What was once an enclosure of Western space betrays only the barest traces of that state. At the novel's close, even those remnants disappear when Heyst sets fire to his bungalow and the contiguous buildings are consumed as well (V 321). When Davidson leaves Samburan, Heyst and the other Westerners are dead, the company buildings are burned to the ground, and Wang alone remains at what was once this Western space, left to claim what little is left. Presumably, the Alfuro people will dismantle the boundary they erected and once again occupy the space that previously housed the mining company, literally transforming Western space into Eastern space. What was once Western space no longer exists, and no barriers remain from those that were erected to establish Western space and divide it from Eastern space.

Like Gentleman Brown and his men, although Mr. Jones, Ricardo, and Pedro could never be mistaken for practitioners of the narrative of benefit's espoused ethical values, their very appearance at the station on Samburan introduces a level of immorality (practiced by these Westerners) in this enclave of Western space. The ethical views of Heyst and Lena largely reflect the conventional morality of the West. The fact that the morality of Heyst and Lena, like Jim's, cannot withstand the assault of the immorality of Mr. Jones and company effectually undermines the power of Western morality, again revealing it to be a segment of a social contract, a contingent truth rather than a transcendental truth. The presence of a lack of Western morality in this Western space transforms it such that it no longer reflects one of the primary values of the narrative of benefit, and this absence directly leads to the ultimate annihilation of the station. As happens in *Lord Jim*, at the close of *Victory*, the complete physical degeneration of the station removes the physical boundaries between Eastern and Western space on Samburan, while the defeat of Western morals and their degeneration (embodied by Mr. Jones and company) has already erased the metaphorical boundaries between Eastern and Western space.

Unlike the trading posts at Samburan and Patusan, the post in Sambir in *Almayer's Folly* and *An Outcast of the Islands* begins with clear distinctions between Western and Eastern space, but like the posts in Patusan and Samburan those distinctions eventually disappear. At the outset of *An Outcast of the Islands*, Lingard & Co.'s trading station is distinguished from the rest of Sambir by the fence surrounding the compound but also by its geography, with the trading station located on one side of the Pantai River and Lakamba's compound (and later Abdulla's as well) on the other side. These physical demarcations reinforce the white men's perceived distinction between the Western space of the station and the Eastern space outside. Initially, the trading station is a thriving monopoly, a model of Western capitalism and the envy of other traders in the archipelago (*e.g.*, OI 88). When Willems betrays Lingard and reveals his secret passage into Sambir, however, the state of the station alters drastically, as do the boundaries between Eastern and Western space in the region.

By the opening of *Almayer's Folly*, the station resembles the state of Stein's trading post under Cornelius's direction. Willems is dead, and

Lingard has long since disappeared, leaving Almayer as the sole Western trader. He has no goods to trade, nor can he do any trade because Abdulla has usurped Lingard's trading partners from among the local population. As a result of this quandary, the trading station, again like Stein's station under Cornelius, begins to reflect in its physical state the disappearance of the borders between the Western space of the station and the surrounding space of Sambir. The company office has fallen into disrepair:

> Books open with torn pages bestrewed the floor; other books lay about grimy and black, looking as if they had never been opened. Account books. … In the middle of the room the big office desk, with one of its legs broken, careened over like the hull of a stranded ship; most of the drawers had fallen out, disclosing heaps of paper yellow with age and dirt. … The desk, the paper, the torn books, and the broken shelves, all under a thick coat of dust. The very dust and bones of a dead and gone business. (AF 157)

Most telling is the state of the house Almayer had begun building (dubbed Almayer's folly). Because of the change in trading fortunes, the house remains forever unfinished, gradually disintegrating along the way. When late in the novel, like Heyst, Almayer sets fire to his home and the company buildings and moves into Almayer's folly, he literally extinguishes the primary demarcations between Eastern and Western space at the station, the sole remnants of the West being Almayer's folly and Almayer himself. When Almayer then turns to opium and slowly destroys himself, he mirrors the degeneration and disappearance of the remnants of Lingard & Co. With the incomplete state and gradual disintegration of Almayer's folly, by the close of the novel, all that remains of the West is the wreck of the unfinished house, which will soon be subsumed into the surrounding space.

The seeds of the breakdown of barriers between Eastern and Western space in Sambir exist, though, well before Willems's betrayal. Like Cornelius in *Lord Jim*, Almayer marries a Malay woman, and so their jointly-held property and the station they occupy are both Eastern and Western. More important is the progressive erosion of the narrative of benefit throughout *Almayer's Folly* and *An Outcast of the Islands*, which consistently undermines the traders' efforts to segregate Western from non-Western space. The novels make no direct reference to the narrative of benefit, but they continually imply Willems's and Almayer's belief in it, primarily through their dogmatic insistence on racial superiority and its accompanying justification for their colonial enterprises.

As suggested above, a particularly important element of Western superiority is the belief in their ethical superiority. Conrad expresses the stereotypical portrayal of the lack of ethics of the non-West, for example, when he reveals Babalatchi's admiration of Omar el Badavi's moral code: "He was brave and bloodthirsty without any affection, and he hated the white men who interfered with the manly pursuits of throat-cutting, kidnapping, slave-dealing, and fire-raising, that were the only possible occupation for a true man of the sea" (OI 43). Lakamba holds similar views, only refraining from poisoning Patalolo and killing Lingard and Almayer (OI 46-47) because Babalatchi persuades him that doing so would be impractical and politically unwise (not because such acts would be immoral). Similarly, Almayer, when thinking of his wife's reaction to his sending Nina away to school, believes, "She will poison me, … well aware of that easy and final manner of solving the social, political, or family problems in Malay life" (AF 22). The narrative of benefit holds that the Westerners who have sought to establish Western space in the non-West create a space within which high ethical values reign and that those values benefit non-Westerners by disseminating values contrary to those held by individuals such as Omar, Lakamba, and Babalatchi, whom Westerners see as embodying the immorality of their culture.

Unlike in *Victory* and *Lord Jim*, though, the unethical actions of Almayer and Willems themselves (rather than that of the Western outlaws of *Lord Jim* and *Victory*) aid in revealing the illusory boundaries between the Western space of the trading post and the Eastern space of surrounding Sambir. In effect, the unethical behavior of the traders at Lingard & Co's trading post voids the idea of Western ethical superiority and differences between the supposed Western space of the station and the non-Western space of the rest of Sambir.

Willems revels in his state of superiority; he delights in the "awe-struck respect" of his mixed heritage wife and her family, which "completed his existence in a perpetual assurance of unquestionable superiority" (OI 7). Ironically, Willems does nothing to justify these feelings. In truth, just the opposite; he does not benefit the local population except his family in a minor economic manner, and even this benefit benefits his ego more than his family, whom he continually humiliates with his superior attitude. Further dismantling the narrative of benefit is Willems's failure to live up to the ethical standards that the narrative espouses when he embezzles from Hudig, abandons his wife, and takes Aïssa as his mistress. Willems exacerbates this failure when he later betrays Lingard. Despite his ethical failures, Willems continues to consider himself superior to the local population. After his first encounter with Aïssa, Willems's "first impulse was that of revolt. He would never go back there. Never!" (OI 58). Because of his racial biases, he feels he has degraded himself by beginning a relationship with a Malay woman.

Almayer similarly considers himself superior to the Malays. He too feels degraded by his match with his Malay wife, and he too is guilty of unethical behavior and betrayal, both counter to the ethical values insisted upon by the narrative of benefit. Late in the novel, when Almayer catches up to his daughter Nina, who is fleeing with Dain Maroola, he threatens to summon the Dutch authorities who are pursuing Maroola. At that point, Nina accuses her father not only of hypocrisy but of unethical behavior: "you that cannot be true to your own countrymen. Only a few days ago you were selling the powder for their destruction; now you want to give up to them the man that yesterday you called your friend" (AF 142). Almayer acts unethically when selling gunpowder that resulted in the death of several Dutchmen and was meant to result in the death of many more; then he threatens to give Dain Maroola over to the Dutch authorities. In the space of a few days, Almayer betrays both his fellow Europeans and his friend. The narrative of benefit suggests that within the Western space they inhabit at the trading post superior ethics are enacted, contrary to the absence of such ethics in the Eastern space surrounding them, but the acts of betrayal and immorality by both Willems and Almayer reveal instead a space absent of the ethics of the narrative of benefit.

As bad as Willems's actions are, Almayer's are worse still. Like Willems, Almayer insists upon his racial superiority. Early on, while thinking of his agreement with Dain Maroola, Almayer muses, "Trusting to Malays was poor work; but then even Malays have some sense and understand their own interest" (AF 12). Furthermore, Almayer only marries his wife, Lingard's adopted daughter, because Lingard promises his wealth as an inheritance. Almayer accepts the arrangement but is at the same time "consciousness of shame that he a white man" would marry a Malay woman, and he also "had a vague idea of shutting her up somewhere, anywhere. … Easy enough to dispose of a Malay woman, a slave, after all, … ceremony or no ceremony" (AF 9). Almayer's marrying solely for an inheritance does not violate the ethics espoused in the narrative of benefit as such, but his plans to abandon his wife, whom he considers no more than Lingard's captured slave, certainly does go against that ethical code, although Almayer feels justified in such a determination because his wife is a Malay woman. Certainly, his wife experiences no benefit from the narrative of benefit.

Ironically, in both *Almayer's Folly* and *An Outcast of the Islands*, despite Almayer's and Willems's belief of racial superiority, the Malays continually show themselves to be superior to the Westerners. They outwit, outthink, and outmanœuver the Westerners, often through the Westerners' own failure to exhibit the ethical edicts of their own narrative of benefit. More revealing, though, is the clear show of ethical superior Dain Maroola demonstrates. Throughout the book, like Karain and Dain Waris, he carries himself with dignity, and late in the novel shows himself to be Almayer's ethical superior. He declines to kill Almayer after foiling Almayer's attempt to shoot him and asks, "Am I a wild beast that you should try to kill me suddenly and in the dark, Tuan Almayer?" (AF 139). Despite Almayer's frenzied attempt to murder him (because Almayer thinks he is racially inferior and therefore an unworthy mate for Nina), Dain Maroola disarms Almayer and then calmly calls on him to discuss the situation reasonably: "Now we may talk, Tuan. It is easy to send out death, but can your wisdom recall the life?" (AF 139). Dain Maroola dramatically demonstrates his superiority, entirely undermining the narrative of benefit that drives so much of Almayer's action and that insists that Almayer is Dain Maroola's ethical and rational superior. Nina symbolically shows this same reversal of superiority. She is of mixed heritage, but Almayer, who holds tenaciously to his conviction of racial superiority, sees her only as white (while the other Westerners see her as only Malay). He plans for their removal to Europe (while simultaneously for abandoning his wife), but Nina chooses instead her Malay heritage, rejecting all elements of the West (except for her father) and selecting a Malay man for her husband because the non-Western world embraces her while the Western world rejects her.

Nina's choice becomes the impetus for Almayer's greatest ethical failing when he disowns his daughter. Almayer fails because of his dogmatic desire to codify racial superiority, in effect to maintain as Western space the circumscribed space he inhabits at the station in Sambir. Conrad could convey no more profound critique of the narrative of benefit (with its an unwavering conviction of racial superiority) than when Almayer disowns Nina (AF 152). The tragedy culminates when he determines that "only one idea remained clear and definite – not to forgive her; only one vivid desire – to forget her" (AF 152). Beginning the process, "he fell on his hands and knees, and, creeping along the sand, erased carefully with his hand all traces of Nina's footsteps. He piled up small heaps of sand, leaving behind him a line of miniature graves right down to the water" (AF 154). Unwittingly, in attempting to eradicate all evidence of Nina, Almayer succeeds only in eradicating the narrative of benefit's insistence of racial superiority and the Western demarcations it represents. With Almayer's choosing the narrative of benefit over love for his daughter, Conrad, who invariably questions those who choose ideas over individuals,[6] removes any hint of superiority, and Almayer's subsequent degeneration becomes merely a symbolic reflection of the failure of the narrative of benefit and the failure of this enclave of the Western world to show itself to be superior to the non-Western world and to establish distinctions between Western and non-Western space.

As the novel comes to a close, Almayer has abandoned Nina and has been abandoned by his wife (along with the rest of the local population), and with Almayer's home and the company offices destroyed and Almayer's folly disintegrating into the surrounding scenery, the station has become a "great empty space" (AF 159). Almayer's death completes the dismantling of the barriers between Eastern and Western space that Lingard had erected when he established the trading post. No Westerners and no elements of Western space remain amidst the ruins of Almayer's folly. Like Stein's station and the Tropical Coal Belt Company, Lingard & Co.'s station has merged with the Eastern space from which it had initially attempted to separate itself and is once again part of the silent, empty space of Sambir.

Even more dramatic, at the outset of "An Outpost of Progress," the sounds and signs of the West are starkly separate from their absence outside the outpost. The company director, Kayerts, and Carlier converse enthusiastically about the outpost and its future. Even after the director departs, the traders continue to converse extensively and make plans for the station. When Carlier notices "the river, the forests, the impenetrable bush that seemed to cut off the station from the rest of the world" (OP 78), he emphasizes the distinction between the station's metaphorical Western space and the surrounding African space. Once left to themselves, the traders continue to reinforce this spatial distinction: "The first day they were very active, pottering about with hammers and nails and red calico,

[6] For more on this idea, see my *Conrad and Impressionism* (145-58) and my "Meet the new boss / Same as the old boss."

to put up curtains, make their house habitable and pretty; resolved to settle down comfortably to their new life" (OP 80). This sort of activity progresses as the African workers at the station "were mustered every morning and told off to different tasks – grass-cutting, fence-building, tree-felling, &c., &c." (OP 87). This process is intended to transform African space into Western space. Within the outpost itself, the difference between Western and African space is maintained. The traders live and work in structures constructed after Western methods and models, while their African workers "lived in straw huts on the slope of a ravine overgrown with reedy grass, just behind the station buildings" (OP 87). Unlike the other station buildings, no "grass-cutting, fence-building, tree-felling, &c., &c." occurs around these straw huts. Correspondingly, Western ethics and social order are also meant to transform African space into Western space.

After a time, though, the outpost grows increasingly wild. The narrator notes, "Rank grass began to sprout over the courtyard" (OP 93), and Makola assesses, "Station in very bad order" (OP 88). This transformation accompanies an increasing absence of sound (*e.g.*, OP 88, 90, 92) and an increasing absence of meaning, as the traders correspondingly move increasingly further from their Western sensibilities. In this state, the outpost has become less a Western space than an African "void" (OP 92), as demarcations between Western and African space grow progressively indistinguishable. Accompanying this movement – this gradual receding from the West – is an inevitable movement toward a space empty of Western identity, as embedded in its sound, values, and rituals of social relations.

Along with the progressive breaking down of Western and African spatial boundaries, as the physical space of the station comes more and more to resemble the surrounding African space, Conrad also removes the boundaries separating Western from African space by chronicling the decivilizing of its Western traders such that the space they inhabit no longer reflects Western values but rather a space empty of all such values.

The narrative of benefit is present at the outset of the tale. The traders early on find a newspaper that discussed "'Our Colonial Expansion' in high-flown language. It spoke much of the rights and duties of civilization, of the sacredness of the civilizing work, and extolled the merits of those who went about bringing light, and faith and commerce to the dark places of the earth" (OP 83). This view posits a decided difference between Western and African space, and Kayerts and Carlier enthusiastically embrace the civilizing narrative that they are engaged in improving and benefitting the Africans. Carlier goes so far as to predict that in a hundred years "there will be perhaps a town here. Quays, and warehouses, and barracks, and – and – billiard-rooms. Civilization, my boy, and virtue – and all. And then, chaps will read that two good fellows, Kayerts and Carlier, were the first civilized men to live in this very spot!" (OP 83). Kayerts concurs, believing that "it is a consolation to think of that" (OP 83). In this, the narrative of benefit establishes a wide gap between Western and African space, and the traders envision a non-Western space eventually transformed into a Western space – but as the story unfolds the exact opposite occurs.

The catalyst for the traders' departure from Western values and an accompanying departure from Western space comes when Makola trades some of the station's African workers for a large lot of ivory (OP 88-89). Initially horrified to learn of this transaction, Kayerts and Carlier "both sat in silence for a while. Then Kayerts related his conversation with Makola. Carlier said nothing. At the midday meal they ate very little. They hardly exchanged a word that day. A great silence seemed to lie heavily over the station and press on their lips" (OP 90). The silence that the traders exhibit mirrors the silence they perceive in African space, suggesting a conflation rather than a distinction between Western and African spaces. This conflation takes place because this Western space has become African space through the slave trading that has now become part of the space of the station. Leopold II's primary stated purpose for desiring the Congo territory for a colony was to disseminate Western values. He particularly promoted abolishing the Congo slave trade.[7] As a result, slavery became a particularly prominent point of comparison that Westerners used to distinguish Western space from African space. In the end, though, Kayerts and

[7]At the Berlin Conference (1884–85), in order to convince the Western colonial powers to allow him to take control of the Congo region, Leopold II focused extensively on the narrative of benefit, especially highlighting his desire to eradicate the slave trade in central Africa (see Hochschild 84–87). In reality, the promise to abolish slavery was primarily propaganda, as the company's agents routinely looked the other way concerning the slave trade, only opposing it when it benefitted them, and sometimes themselves engaging in the slave trade along with other practices akin to it, such as varying degrees of forced labor (Hochschild 119–20; 129–35). Adam Hochschild discusses the trading company's purchasing slaves to carry out company work (129–30), and George Washington Williams recounts first-hand that the company employed Zanzibar slaves, sending their wages to the slaves' owners (*Railroad* 8-9).

Carlier maintain their silence concerning this incident and thus offer their tacit consent: "Kayerts hesitated at first – was afraid of the Director. 'He has seen worse things done on the quiet,' maintained Carlier, with a hoarse laugh. 'Trust him! He won't thank you if you blab. He is no better than you or me. Who will talk if we hold our tongues? There is nobody here'" (OP 93). Nothing prevents them from hiding this slave trade ("Who will talk if we hold our tongues?"). Once the traders choose silence over speech, they align themselves with silence rather than the sound that previously dominated the station. More important, though, they themselves have become slave traders, making themselves complicit in Makola's transaction. Carlier later accuses Kayerts: "You are a slave-dealer. I am a slave-dealer. There's nothing but slave-dealers in this cursed country" (OP 94). The station has now become a slave-trading station, a space engaged in a practice that had long-since been abolished throughout Europe and its colonies. Given slavery's status as a primary target of the narrative of benefit and a touchstone topic in Europe, the station's transformation into a slave-trading space places it prominently outside Western spatial and experiential boundaries.

After the slave trade, Kayerts and Carlier regress, and a corresponding emptying of sound, morals, and social values accompanies the station's inexorable spatial divorce from the West: "The bell never rang now. Days passed, silent, exasperating, and slow. When the two men spoke, they snarled; and their silences were bitter" (OP 93-94). The traders and the station become engulfed in silence and rarely speak. This situation fully devolves: first when Carlier, "in a fit of rage," insists on "the necessity of exterminating" the Africans, while Kayerts simply "mooned about silently" (OP 93), and then afterward when Kayerts and Carlier fight over the diminishing store of sugar. Carlier begins by "kicking at the door furiously, howling" at Kayerts, "If you don't bring out that sugar, I will shoot you at sight, like a dog" (OP 95). This state exists because "there was no power on earth outside of themselves" (OP 85). There are no external checks on these representatives of the West in the surrounding emptiness. Unlike in the West, no laws, powers, or individuals prevent Carlier from shooting Kayerts if he so chooses, just as nothing prevents them from engaging in slave trading. When Kayerts tries to assert his authority as station chief, Carlier rejects Western social order and counters, "Who's chief? There's no chief here. There's nothing here: there's nothing but you and I" (OP 94). In other words, nothing exists outside themselves, nothing to enforce any roles, hierarchies, morals, or social structures of power. The outpost has become a space of negation.

During the ensuing struggle, Kayerts asks himself, "What was it all about? … What did they quarrel about? That sugar! How absurd!" (OP 95), but he realizes this too late as the two collide during the scuffle and Kayerts' revolver accidentally discharges: "A loud explosion took place between them; A roar of red fire, thick smoke: and Kayerts, deafened and blinded, … Then he heard a crashing fall on the other side of the house, as if somebody had tumbled headlong over a chair. … then silence. Nothing more happened. … The other man made no sound" (OP 96). The explosion pushes both men into states of silence, Kayerts momentarily deafened and Carlier killed. As with the slave trading, silence then envelopes Carlier's death when Makola says to Kayerts, "He died of fever. Yes, I think he died of fever. Bury him to-morrow" (OP 97), and Kayerts, as with the slave trade, tacitly consents. Nothing prevents Kayerts from concealing the circumstances surrounding Carlier's death, just as nothing prevented the traders from concealing the slave trade. The following day Kayerts completes the circle of silence engulfing this former sound-filled Western space when in "the mist penetrating, enveloping, and silent" (OP 98), he hears the sound of the Western steamboat's whistle heralding its arrival and hangs himself, permanently silencing himself and imposing silence upon all those who find him. No one will ever know what actually happened. The story ends and is silent concerning what befalls the station thereafter.

This dissolving of distinctions between Western and non-Western space progresses even more inexorably in *Heart of Darkness*. Like "An Outpost of Progress," the trading stations in *Heart of Darkness* resemble not Western spaces but instead the surrounding African space, but whereas the station in "An Outpost of Progress" begins in sound and moves toward silence and begins as Western space and moves toward African space, from the very outset of Marlow's journey, the stations in *Heart of Darkness* have already been largely emptied of Western sound and space, and Marlow's tale reveals itself to be his gradually recognition of the extent of this state. This discovery will eventually come to have a profound effect on his view of the West itself.

When Marlow arrives at the company's outer station, he perceives "houses on a hill, others with iron roofs, amongst a waste of excavations," a "scene of inhabited devastation" (HD 67). He sees "a boiler wallowing the grass," then encounters "an undersized railway-truck lying there on its back with its wheels in the air. One was off. The thing looked as dead as the carcass of some animal," and he comes upon "more pieces of decaying machinery" (HD 67). Shortly thereafter, Marlow discovers that "a lot of imported drainage-pipes for the settlement had been tumbled" into a narrow ravine and that "there wasn't one that was not broken. It was a wanton smash-up" (HD 71), yet another image of waste and inefficiency. The image of the railway-truck looking "as dead as the carcass of some animal" and the general waste and inefficiency suggest a space removed from its Western models, which prided themselves on their efficiency and order. Marlow concludes that except for the chief accountant's superficial connection to Western space through his Western attire, "Everything else in the station was in a muddle, – heads, things, buildings" (HD 71). Like the station at the conclusion of "An Outpost of Progress," rather than a space of order, meaning, and efficiency, one meant to embody Western space, the outer station is a space absent of these values: in effect – an empty space.

The company's central station is similar. Marlow first finds it lying "on a back water surrounded by scrub and forest, with a pretty border of smelly mud on one side, and on the three others enclosed by a crazy fence of rushes. A neglected gap was all the gate it had" (HD 75). Even more than the outer station, the central station from the outset appears to be more African than Western space because of its close proximity to the forest and because one border is "smelly mud" while the other three form a fence made out of rushes. Rather than the constructed boundaries Marlow would find in the West, the central station rises out of its African surroundings. Also, like the overturned railway truck at the outer station, Marlow compares the damaged steamboat to the "carcass of some big river animal" (HD 82), in this way again drawing the space of the station closer to the African space enfolding it.

Further drawing Western space into African space, the company's central station exhibits the same inefficiency and waste that permeate the outer station, but the central station augments these aspects by introducing an even more prominent element of absurdity than was evident at the outer station (thereby emphasizing its absence of sense). For example, prior to Marlow's arriving, the steamboat embarks without a trained sailor piloting it and shortly thereafter is incompetently sunk. Adding to the absurdity, the station manager expects Marlow, without even having inspected the damage, to estimate how long the repairs will require (HD 77). Yet further exacerbating this situation is the significant delay in repair, resulting partly from the lack of rivets and partly from failing to have them brought from the outer station (although there are boxes of them there).[8]

The inefficiency surrounding the traders is even more revealing. One would expect that they would have some occupation, but Marlow recounts that they merely "wandered here and there with their absurd long staves in their hands, like a lot of faithless pilgrims bewitched inside a rotten fence" (HD 77). Conrad takes this description a step further with the brickmaker. His job, of course, is to make bricks, but Marlow notes that "there wasn't a fragment of a brick anywhere in the station, and he had been there more than a year – waiting. It seems he could not make bricks without something, I don't know what – straw maybe. Anyway, it could not be found there and as it was not likely to be sent from Europe" (HD 79). The lack of bricks is the kind of inefficiency Marlow experienced at the outer station, but the brickmaker's maintaining his role as brickmaker in the absence of any apparent possibility of obtaining the missing matter adds an element of absurdity, as does the stout man with moustaches' attempt to douse the fire in the supply shed. He ran past Marlow and "dipped about a quart of water [out of the river] and tore back again" toward the fire. Marlow notices, though, that "there was a hole in the bottom of his pail" (HD 78). Inefficiency and absurdity abound here. Marlow assesses that the shed "had gone off like a box of matches. It had been hopeless from the very first" (HD 78), but even had there been a chance of extinguishing the flames, dousing the shed with quart-sized pails of water, one at a time, while running back and forth between the river and the blaze, could hardly have accomplished the task – even if there had been no hole in the pail. Rather than demonstrating efficiency, order, and purpose – as is demanded of Western space – the central station, like the outer station, is the exact opposite: a space with no efficiency, no order, no purpose – a space even more clearly than the outer station showing itself to be a space of absence.

The collapsing of Western and non-Western spatial distinctions is most pronounced, though, at the inner station:

[8] Marlow reveals, "Rivets I wanted. There were cases of them down at the coast – cases – piled up – burst – split! You kicked a loose rivet at every second step in that station-yard on the hillside. Rivets had rolled into the grove of death. You could fill your pockets with rivets for the trouble of stooping down – and there wasn't one rivet to be found where it was wanted" (HD 84).

> A long decaying building on the summit was half buried in the high grass; the large holes in the peaked roof gaped black from afar; the jungle and the woods made a background. There was no enclosure or fence of any kind; but there had been one apparently, for near the house half-a-dozen slim posts remained in a row, roughly trimmed, and with their upper ends ornamented with round carved balls. The rails, or whatever there had been between, had disappeared. Of course the forest surrounded all that. (HD 113-14)

Various parts of the central station were constructed out of the African surroundings. This effect appears still more prominently at the inner station. The station's "ruined roof, the long mud wall peeping above the grass" (HD 119), along with its high grass (like Kayert's and Carlier's station once in decline) and its closely encompassing forest, suggest a station embodying African rather than Western space. Marlow refers to it as Kurtz's "empty and desolate station" (HD 89). In fact, the Russian says that Kurtz often abandoned the station for long periods (HD 118), leaving it with no Western presence at all. Most telling, though, is the fence, which is at once both absent and present. It is unclear whether a fence ever actually encircled the station. Marlow assumes that the posts around it are part of a now-decayed fence (an element of the station's being reabsorbed into African space), but Marlow later discovers that what had appeared from a distance to be "carved balls" mounted atop the posts (HD 114) are in reality severed heads: "black, dried, sunken, with closed eyelids" (HD 120). The existence of these heads may signal that Kurtz and his follows have been practicing ritual cannibalism,[9] but whether signs of cannibalism or simply a stark warning to "rebels" (HD 121), they remove the inner station from any Western model and align it with a practice Westerners

[9] Herbert Ward recalls, "The skulls of the victims to [*sic*] cannibalism are always exposed in some prominent position in the village, as a mark of the importance of the chief. Sometimes a house will be decorated with human skulls placed in rows, on small platforms built for the purpose, on the four sides of the house. In other places the skulls are hung about in bunches on poles" (119-20). Thomas Heazle Parke recounts, "After a difficult march we reached a village. As usual, posts were stuck up around it with skulls on top; one of these was distinctly 'recent,' as there was still some flesh on it, and its appearance at once developed the idea that its unhappy owner had been an item on the menu at a cannibal banquet lately held by the inhabitants" (84). Sanuel Langford Hinde reveals that in N'Gandu, a village of ten to fifteen thousand people, "The top of every tree in this palisade was crowned with a human skull" (91). And Guy Burrows relates, "The skulls [of those killed and eaten] are stuck up on posts around the village" (154).

associated solely with the non-Western world, thereby merging Western space with non-Western space.

The station is also closely linked to African space because of its proximity to the local village but more so because the Africans inhabit both spaces, coming and going freely. Unlike the Africans at the outer and central stations, who are exclusively connected to the company, those at the inner station do not belong to the trading company but are followers of Kurtz, and by this time, Kurtz himself has also come to see himself as outside company boundaries, informing Marlow, "This lot of ivory now is really mine. The Company did not pay for it. I collected it myself at a very great personal risk" (HD 138). Kurtz argues that his recent ivory collecting was not accomplished as a company trader but rather as an independent agent.

More important, though, is Kurtz's role as African deity, which transforms the station from a space of Western trade to one of African worship, as the station and local village merge. As such, the inner station is the terminus where distinctions between the metaphorical Western space of the stations and the surrounding African space are erased. The central station manager codifies this metamorphosis when he abandons this outpost, concluding, "The district is closed to us for a time" (HD 125). When the steamboat leaves, the station is populated by some one thousand Africans with no Westerners present. This former Western space has wholly merged with African space, and the two are now a single space, the same silent and empty space Marlow encounters throughout Africa.

As with the newspaper article in "An Outpost of Progress," Marlow's aunt articulates the narrative of benefit. When Marlow obtains his job in the Congo, his aunt sees him as "one of the Workers, with a capital – you know. Something like an emissary of light, something like a lower sort of apostle" and insists that he will be "weaning those ignorant millions from their horrid ways" (HD 62-63). Marlow quickly discovers, though, that the narrative of benefit, the company's justification for its actions and for the presence of its stations, is merely a "philanthropic pretence" (HD 80), that the narrative of "improving knowledge" (HD 85) is empty sound, in other words – silence. No improving occurs;[10] no Western system of ethics,

[10] See, for instance, the African fireman aboard the steamboat who is taught not the scientific theory behind steam power and its workings but is told instead "that should the water in that transparent thing disappear, the evil spirit inside the boiler would get angry through the greatness of his thirst, and take a terrible vengeance" (HD 95).

efficiency, or order emerges – only exploitation. Like Kayerts and Carlier, the Western traders in *Heart of Darkness* cannot maintain their Western trappings once removed from the West, and the trading stations become spaces of literal and metaphorical emptiness.

Like the ethical devolution that evolves at the trading stations in *Victory*, *Lord Jim*, *Almayer's Folly*, *An Outcast of the Islands*, and "An Outpost of Progress," a similar state exists at the stations in *Heart of Darkness*, except that before Marlow ever arrives, the devolution is already accomplished. The sole exception to the "inhabited devastation" (HD 67) of the company's outer station is found in its chief accountant. Marlow describes him wearing "a high starched collar, white cuffs, a light alpaca jacket, snowy trousers, a clear necktie, and varnished boots. No hat. Hair parted, brushed, oiled, under a green-lined parasol held in a big white hand. He was amazing, and had a penholder behind his ear" (HD 70). Only in appearance, though, does the chief accountant resemble his counterparts in the West: he soon shows himself to be little more than a human calculator, incapable of human compassion or moral thinking. When Marlow asks how he maintains his appearance, he replies, "I've been teaching one of the native women about the station. It was difficult. She had a distaste for the work" (HD 71). Not reaching the level of Makola's slave trading, the chief accountant nevertheless clearly engages in forced labor.

Even more troubling, he exhibits no sympathy for the dying agent who is moved into his office, complaining instead that the "groans of this sick person distract my attention. And without that it is extremely difficult to guard against clerical errors in this climate" (HD 71; see also 72). Later, when a noisy caravan of African carriers arrives, the accountant fumes, "When one has got to make correct entries, one comes to hate those savages – hate them to the death" (HD 72). His annoyance at the dying agent's groans and his utter lack of compassion toward him, along with his distinct desire that the Africans were dead simply because their noise might distract him from "making correct entries of perfectly correct transactions" (HD 72), remove him from the priorities and ethical code espoused in the Western world.

The chief accountant is not alone in his divorce from the Western code of ethics. Other elements at the outer station uncover this absence. Almost immediately after arriving, Marlow observes a chain gang: "They were called criminals, and the outraged law, like the bursting shells, had come to them, an insoluble mystery from the sea" (HD 68). Marlow refers to their incarceration as "an insoluble mystery" and thus clearly posits his perception that this action lies outside normal Western ethics. But Marlow's critique does not end there. Along with the mysterious reason for their incarceration, he "could see every rib, the joints of their limbs were like knots in a rope; each had an iron collar on his neck, and all were connected together with a chain whose bights swung between them, rhythmically clinking." Furthermore, "all their meagre breasts panted together, the violently dilated nostrils quivered, the eyes stared stonily uphill. They passed me within six inches, without a glance, with that complete, deathlike indifference of unhappy savages" (HD 68). Regardless of their supposed crime, their physical condition, a product of their punishment, is presented as beyond the bounds of what would be considered permissible punishment in the West.

Marlow steps into a shady grove to "let that chain-gang get out of sight" (HD 68), when he discovers an even more horrifying scene. African workers were "brought from all the recesses of the coast in all the legality of time contracts, lost in uncongenial surroundings, fed on unfamiliar food, they sickened, became inefficient, and were then allowed to crawl away and rest" (HD 69). Marlow discloses, "They were dying slowly – it was very clear" (HD 69). Besides the existence of a space that would be unacceptable in the West, Marlow further removes the boundaries between Western and non-Western space when he notices that one of the dying Africans has "a bit of white worsted round his neck." Marlow concludes that this object "looked startling round his black neck, this bit of white thread from beyond the seas" (HD 70). This "bit of white worsted" symbolizes the West strangling Africa and correspondingly brings together Western and non-Western space in this "grove of death" (HD 72). The grove results solely from Western actions, but it also joins the West to Africa in the physical tie of the white worsted round the African's neck. At this moment, an element of the West and another of Africa occupy the same ontological space.

Even more than the company's outer station, its central station represents a space of moral absence. On the two-hundred mile overland trek to the station, Marlow notes that "the population had cleared out a long time ago" and suggests that if they were in England and a lot mysterious black men were "catching the yokels right and left to carry heavy loads for them, I fancy every farm and cottage thereabouts would get empty very soon" (HD 73). In other words, the local African population had abandoned their villages to avoid being conscripted into forced labor, something that had clearly occurred at one point.

Upon arriving at the central station, Marlow observes that "the first glance at the place was enough to let you see the flabby devil was running that show" (HD 75). Earlier, Marlow described this "flabby devil" as a "weak-eyed devil of rapacious and pitiless folly" (HD 68), a metaphorical embodiment of values antithetical to the Western narrative of benefit. Like the cruelty occurring at the outer station, Marlow recounts that the traders savagely beat one of the Africans after the supply shed goes up in flames: "They said he had caused the fire in some way; be that as it may, he was screeching most horribly. I saw him, later, for several days, sitting in a bit of shade looking very sick and trying to recover himself" (HD 78). Despite this graphic description, Marlow does not do justice to the severity of the punishment, which would have been carried out with a *chicote*, a whip-like instrument made of hippopotamus hide, and which sometimes caused the death of the victim.[11] Nevertheless, when the beaten African later groans, the stout man with moustaches reveals a typical lack of compassion, complaining, "What a row the brute makes! Serve him right. Transgression – punishment – bang! Pitiless, pitiless. That's the only way" (HD 81). As with the chain gang at the outer station, even were the African guilty of setting the fire (which does not seem certain), the punishment far overreaches the offence.[12] Once more, a gap is apparent between the code of ethics touted in the West and what actually transpires at its stations in the non-West. The stations seem to proceed with no ethical structure at all and thus have removed themselves from one of the primary accouterments of Western space, one the West consistently used to discriminate Western from non-Western space.

At the central station, Marlow first articulates the origins of this moral absence, a state that had been increasingly apparent from the very moment he encountered Africa in connection with the company. When Fresleven some months earlier "mercilessly" beat an African chief over a

[11] See, for example, E. J. Glave's detailed description of this punishment ("Cruelty" 703), as well as accounts of deaths resulting from this practice in J. Rose Troup (248) and George Washington Williams (*Open Letter* 13).

[12] Marlow further underscores his assessment of the punishment by referring to the lost supplies as "trash" (HD 78). In other words, Marlow thinks that the African has been beaten over lost "trash."

misunderstanding about two hens (HD 58), he was acting outside conventional Western ethical boundaries. Fresleven is killed during this incident, not because of legal consequences for his actions but because the chief's son is trying to protect his father. In other words, in the West, Fresleven would not have mercilessly beat anyone over a misunderstanding about some hens without incurring severe consequences, but those consequences do not exist in Africa.[13] Marlow says of this incident (with significant irony), "Oh, it didn't surprise me in the least to hear this, and at the same time to be told that Fresleven was the gentlest, quietest creature that ever walked on two legs. No doubt he was; but he had been a couple of years already out there engaged in the noble cause" (HD 58). Similarly, when some African carriers accidentally drop Marlow's traveling companion on their journey from the outer station to the central station, the trader "was very anxious for [Marlow] to kill somebody" (HD 74). No Western law would have assigned execution as a permissible punishment for such a failing, and yet Marlow's companion clearly expects that someone should be executed.

Shortly after arriving at the central station, Marlow explains such actions by declaring that "out there there were no external checks" (HD 76), and so, in the absence of "external checks," the Westerners in *Heart of Darkness*, like the traders in "An Outpost of Progress," who are subject to "no power on earth outside of themselves" (OP 85), abandon Western ethical and social order and live completely unrestrained by outside influences. This behavior – in the absence of "external checks" – forms a pattern throughout the tale. When the station manager and his uncle discuss the Russian, for instance, the uncle suggests that the station manager should "get him hanged!" concluding, "Why not? Anything – anything can be done in this country" (HD 89). Were they in Europe, "anything" could not be done; laws, customs, religion, ethics, public opinion, social order, and other similar external restraints would carry considerable consequences for such actions. The brickmaker summarizes the moral emptiness among the traders at the company's stations when he asserts that "he feared neither God nor devil, let alone any mere man" (HD 84). The brickmaker, as do seemingly all other Westerners, acts in the absence of

[13] Of course, racial bias also lies at the back of this and the other similar incidents in *Heart of Darkness*, in that even in Africa Fresleven might incur consequences for beating a white man but not for beating a black man.

any ethical or social restraints.[14] Along with the station's physical state, which discloses a space empty of Western spatial characteristics, the actions of the Western traders disclose a space empty of Western moral characteristics.

Just as the physical space of the inner station is the place most thoroughly antithetical to Western space, so also is its ethical and social atmosphere. The lack of moral behavior that existed at the outer and central stations through a commensurate lack of external restraints multiplies exponentially at the inner station. This absence culminates in Kurtz. The Russian admits that Kurtz raided the surrounding territory searching for ivory and that "there's a good lot of cartridges left even yet." Kurtz was able to do so with the help of some local Africans because "they adored him" (HD 118). Kurtz's lack of moral sentiment is mirrored in the other traders' attitude toward his actions. Marlow alone censures him, while the central station manager echoes the chief accountant when he exhibits his same lack of compassion and morals. Upon learning of Kurtz's actions, the manager criticizes him, calling his actions "Deplorable!" – but not on ethical grounds. He instead complains that Kurtz "did not see the time was not ripe for vigorous action" and so "upon the whole, the trade will suffer" (HD 125). Murdering Africans to take their ivory, what Marlow called "raid[ing] the country" (HD 118), is for the manager merely "vigorous action" based upon an "unsound method" (HD 125). He is unconcerned that Kurtz devastated communities. In fact, his sole concern is that Kurtz's method has been bad for business. The same is true for the other traders. Far from criticizing Kurtz for killing Africans, they actually replicate Kurtz' behavior. As they prepare to leave the station, a large and

[14] Ironically, the individuals whom the Westerners would have considered as the most savage of savages, the cannibals, are the only characters (besides perhaps Marlow) who exhibit moral behavior in the absence of external restraints. Marlow notes that the cannibals had to have been growing extremely hungry, and he queries, "Why in the name of all the gnawing devils of hunger they didn't go for us – they were thirty to five – and have a good tuck-in for once, amazes me now when I think of it" (HD 100-01). Marlow then muses, "Restraint! What possible restraint? Was it superstition, disgust, patience, fear – or some kind of primitive honour? No fear can stand up to hunger, no patience can wear it out, disgust simply does not exist where hunger is; and as to superstition, beliefs, and what you may call principles, they are less than chaff in a breeze," finally concluding, "And these chaps, too, had no earthly reason for any kind of scruple. Restraint! I would just as soon have expected restraint from a hyena prowling amongst the corpses of a battlefield. But there was the fact facing me – the fact dazzling, to be seen, like the foam on the depths of the sea, like a ripple on an unfathomable enigma" (HD 101).

threatening crowd of Africans arrives. Fearing for their safety, the traders get out their rifles. Before they begin shooting, though, Marlow sounds the steamboat whistle and thereby scatters the crowd in "abject terror,"[15] but the traders had not only been looking to protect themselves, they had also been "anticipating a jolly lark," and one complains disconsolately, "Don't! Don't! You frighten them away" (HD 131). At that point, the traders begin firing into the crowd. Kurtz raided African villages to obtain ivory, but the traders gratuitously shoot the Africans ashore. The rapacity of the Westerners (Kurtz's ivory method for collecting ivory, the manager's attitude toward Kurtz's methods, the traders' shooting Africans for fun) disclose their absolute lack of Western ethical strictures.

Despite this depth of depravity, Kurtz's moral degeneration matters much more in revealing the emptiness of the inner station. Kurtz began his African experience by asserting the narrative of benefit, contending that the company should be improving the state of the Africans: "Each station should be like a beacon on the road towards better things, a centre for trade of course, but also for humanizing, improving, instructing" (HD 89). And in his pamphlet, Kurtz asserts, "By the simple exercise of our will we [Westerners] can exert a power for good practically unbounded" but concludes with a postscript, "scrawled evidently much later, in an unsteady hand" (and reminiscent of Carlier's views, OP 93): "Exterminate all the brutes!" (HD 111). Marlow suggests that "at the end of that moving appeal to every altruistic sentiment it [the postscript] blazed at you, luminous and terrifying, like a flash of lightning in a serene sky" (HD 111). These diametrically opposed sentiments juxtaposing one another underscore just how far this man who had come out to Africa "equipped with moral ideas" (HD 87) has departed from them. Moving from a narrative of benefit to one of extermination shifts the space Kurtz inhabits from a space of Western ethical and social sentiments to one absent of them altogether.

Further demonstrating this emptiness, Kurtz engages in head hunting, a practice that may have been associated with ritual cannibalism but certainly with what Westerners viewed as the polar opposite of Western moral behavior. But even this practice does not represent the *extremis* of Kurtz's total departure from Western values. Kurtz lacks any "innate strength"

[15] Hermann von Wissman recalls, "The impression [of the steam whistle] was again so overpowering that all the natives took to their heels in wild fear, disappearing in the thickets and rushing toward the village" (20).

(HD 110) for performing moral actions in the absence of external restraints and exceeds human boundaries. Despite Kurtz's asserting that he would shoot the Russian if he did not hand over a lot of ivory Kurtz wanted, the Russian insists, "You can't judge Mr Kurtz as you would an ordinary man. No, no, no!" (HD 118). The Russian believes that Kurtz is a kind of *übermensch*, beyond human boundaries and thus warranting different criteria for judging him. And yet Kurtz's pushing beyond moral boundaries does not stop there. Instead, Kurtz goes so far as to aspire to the status of deity. The Africans worship him as a god, and he comes to preside at dances where "unspeakable rites" (presumably human sacrifices) were offered up to Kurtz (HD 111).[16] Allowing himself to be worshipped and offered "unspeakable rites" achieves the extreme limit to which one can depart from a Western system of ethics and social order. As such, Kurtz's actions represent an ultimate moral and social negation. And in reaching the ends of emptiness, Kurtz concurrently embodies the culmination of the numerous other Westerners in the tale who reveal Western ethical and social values to be mere social contracts, empty in the absence of external restraints to enforce them. These values themselves are thus found to be a moral and social blankness, and just as the station in "An Outpost of Progress" becomes a slave-trading space through its traders' slave trading, the stations in *Heart of Darkness* become moral blank spaces through their traders' moral blankness.

References

Burrows, Guy. *The Land of the Pigmies*. New York: Thomas Y. Crowell, 1898.

Conrad, Joseph. *Almayer's Folly*. Edited by Peter Lancelot Mallios. New York: Modern Library, 2002.

———. *The Collected Letters of Joseph Conrad*. Edited by Laurence Davies, et al, 9 vols. Cambridge: Cambridge University Press, 1983–2008.

———. Heart of Darkness. Edited by John G. Peters. Peterborough, Ontario: Broadview Press, 2019.

[16] E. J. Glave relates that among the Bolobo district of the Congo "human sacrifices were constantly made to appease the anger of evil spirits" (*Six Years* 157) and that the large villages around Stanley Pool (now Marebo Pool) "are daily making human sacrifices, either in connection with the death of a chief or for some other ceremonial reason" (*Six Years* 205; see also 229-30). Compare also "An Outpost of Progress": "In his fear, the mild old Gobila offered extra human sacrifices to all the Evil Spirits that had taken possession of his white friends" (OP 92).

———. *Lord Jim*. Edited by Cedric Watts. Peterborough, Ontario: Broadview Press, 2001.

———. *An Outcast of the Islands*. Edited by Cedric Watts. London: Everyman, 1996.

———. "An Outpost of Progress." *Tales of Unrest*. Edited by Allan H. Simmons and J. H. Stape. Cambridge: Cambridge University Press, 2012, pp. 77–99.

———. *Victory*. Edited by Peter Lancelot Mallios. Modern Library, 2003.

———. "Youth: A Narrative." *Youth, Heart of Darkness, The End of the Tether*. Edited by John Lyon. London: Penguin, 1995, pp. 9–43.

Glave, E. J. "Cruelty in the Congo Free State." *Century Magazine*, vol. 54 no. 5, September 1897, pp. 699–715.

———. *Six Years of Adventure in Congo-Land*. London: Sampson Low, Marsden, 1893.

Hinde, Samuel Langford. *The Fall of the Congo Arabs*. London: Methuen, 1897.

Hochschild, Adam. *King Leopold's Ghost: A Story of Greed, Terror, and Heroism in Colonial Africa*. Boston: Houghton Mifflin, 1998.

Parke, Thomas Heazle. *My Personal Experiences in Equatorial Africa*. New York: Charles Scribner's Sons, 1891.

Peters, John G. *Conrad and Impressionism*. Cambridge: Cambridge University Press, 2001.

———. "'Meet the new boss / Same as the old boss': The Politics of Replication and Conrad's Politics of Humanity." *Journal of English Language and Literature*, vol. 66, no. 1, June 2020, pp. 23–42.

Troup, J. Rose. *With Stanley's Rear Column*. London: Chapman and Hall, 1890.

Ward, Herbert. *Five Years with the Congo Cannibals*. London: Chatto & Windus, 1891.

Williams, George Washington. *An Open Letter to His Serene Majesty Leopold*. n.p., [1890].

———. *A Report on the Proposed Congo Railway*. n.p., [1890].

Wissman, Hermann von. *My Second Journey through Equatorial Africa: From the Congo to the Zambezi*. Translated by Minna J. A. Bergmann. London: Chatto & Windus, 1891.

CHAPTER 4

Transformations: Silence, Space, Absence

Abstract This chapter chronicles the transformative journeys Conrad's characters make through their contact with the non-West. Such journeys have as their primary or secondary catalyst the encounter of Western characters with the non-West. These encounters end with the barriers between Western and non-Western space being blurred or disappearing altogether, and, in the process of their journeys, the characters come to reassess their world, their former presuppositions, their biases, and sometimes their conception of the very nature of their being and of the universe.

Keywords Joseph Conrad • Silence • Western space • Non-Western space • Absence • Transformation

In erasing the barriers erected between Western and non-Western space, Conrad is not content merely to recount the process by which the Western stations are revealed to be silent and empty (and correspondingly their traders often de-civilized). Instead, Conrad even more tellingly breaks down Western and non-Western spatial distinctions not just by erasing the spatial demarcations between the space of the Western enclaves in non-Western space but also by breaking down distinctions between the very spaces of the West and the non-West themselves. In the process, Conrad's characters often endure transformational ordeals as a consequence of their encounters with non-Western space.

J. G. Peters, *Silence, Space and Absence in Conrad's Works*,
https://doi.org/10.1007/978-3-031-44910-9_4

Conrad complicates this process by employing a doubling mechanism when he introduces the differing experience between his main characters at the outset of their respective tales and that of their narrators (even when the main character is also the narrator). Jakob Lothe has characterized a difference in *Heart of Darkness* between Marlow the narrator and Marlow the character: "In addition to the frame narrator, the most essential elements of the narrative method of 'Heart of Darkness' are constituted by Marlow's functions as narrator and character" (22), but this dichotomy is apparent not just in Marlow's tales but in most of Conrad's stories, wherever his narrators are also crucial contributors to the occasion of their tale.

When these narrators relate a characters' experiences, the characters have already traversed their life-altering travels, and the narrators disclose the emptiness of both Western and non-Western space that the characters have come to see. In other words, the narrators already know the conclusion to the characters' existential journeys, but they narrate their tales primarily from the characters' perspective (whether employing a first-person or a third-person narrative). This process results in an immediacy of experience for the reader (and the narrator's listeners when they are present). In the conventional narrative, a narrative of retrospect, narrators relate past experiences less as they originally experienced them than as they now perceive them, or they recall past experiences from the vantage of hindsight, while interpreting them along the way. In contrast, a narrative of immediacy presents events as if they were being lived at that very moment. The most effective narrative of immediacy occurs when the narrator's audience participates in the character's experience. When Conrad's first-person narrators engage in a narrative of immediacy, they simply recount the past as if it were the present. For instance, when in *Heart of Darkness*, the central station manager and his uncle berate a "wandering trader – a pestilential fellow, snapping ivory from the natives," Marlow asks himself, "Who was it they were talking about now?" (HD 89). However, Marlow the narrator knows that they are speaking of the Russian, so in querying the identity of the trader, Marlow the narrator is narrating the question that Marlow the character asked himself at the time he overheard the conversation. Consequently, the reader (and Marlow's listeners) wonder the same thing, and only later when Marlow the character meets the Russian do he and his listeners (along with Conrad's readers) discover the identity of this "wandering trader."

Conrad's third-person narrators in a narrative of immediacy behave identically. Like first-person narrators, who have already experienced the events of their tales, third-person narrators have heard or witnessed the events the characters have experienced, but they present the phenomena of their stories as if they were evolving before them. When in *The Secret Agent* Councillor Wurmt enters the waiting room at the embassy, the third-person narrator describes the scene from Verloc's point of view: "Another door opened noiselessly, and Mr Verloc immobilizing his glance in that direction saw at first only black clothes, the bald top of a head, and a drooping dark grey whisker on each side of a pair of wrinkled hands. The person who had entered was holding a batch of papers before his eyes" (SA 48). Because of Verloc's physical location and because Wurmt holds papers in front of him, Verloc sees only part of Wurmt's face. The narrator could have described Wurmt's face (which is, of course, well known to the narrator). Instead, the narrator presents Verloc's partial view of Wurmt and concurrently permits the reader also to see only a portion of Wurmt's face.

In a narrative of immediacy then, readers (and listeners where present) in a sense accompany the characters on their own existential journeys as they experience (at least in part) what the characters experience. The narrators faithfully render the characters' perspective, characters who eventually evolve toward a view that dismisses distinctions between Western and non-Western space.

Before this transformation transpires, Conrad's Westerners first perceive clear distinctions dividing Western space from non-Western space. A correlative between sound-filled and activity-filled Western space and the silent and empty non-Western space includes an analogous disparity between heterogeneous space and homogenous space: space full of demarcations and space empty of them, the former associated with the West and the latter with the non-West. For instance, the descriptions of the London Strand in "Karain" (K 48-49) or the London docks in *"Narcissus"* (NN 248-50) are examples of heterogenous Western space, as are the bustle of the Brussels streets in *Heart of Darkness* (HD 59-60, 135-36) and a teeming London throughout *The Secret Agent*. In contrast, the most striking example of the homogeneity of the non-West is the open ocean, which the narrator of *"Narcissus"* calls "ever changing and ever the same, always monotonous and always imposing" (NN 161). Similarly, the captain in *The Shadow-Line* describes the sea as "monotonous" (SL 107) and complains that there was "no speck on the water, no shape of vapour, no wisp of smoke, no sail, no boat, no stir of humanity, no sign of life, nothing!" (SL 110). The frame narrator in *Heart of Darkness* perhaps most strikingly sums up this situation when he says that “the sea is always the same” (HD 52). But the sea, with its lack of demarcations, is only the most obvious embodiment of the distinction between homogenous non-Western space and heterogenous Western space.

Non-Western spaces, such as Africa, Patusan, and Russia are similarly described as homogenous. Marlow speaks of Patusan’s “dark waves of continuous tree-tops” and notes that a “brooding gloom lay over this vast and monotonous landscape; the light fell on it as if into an abyss” (LJ 250). Patusan for Marlow is a homogenous landscape, which appears to him as a uniform space of “continuous tree-tops” in a “vast and monotonous landscape.” Even more emphatic, as Marlow travels down Africa’s coast, he claims, “Every day the coast looked the same” (HD 64). In perceiving a “vast and monotonous landscape” in Patusan and an unchanging coast in Africa, Marlow perceives homogenous non-Western expanses – ones empty of distinguishing demarcations. Even more graphically, the Western teacher of languages, the unnamed narrator in *Under Western Eyes* (1911), describes Razumov’s perception of the space of Russia as “levelling everything under its uniform whiteness” (UWE 71). More than Marlow’s vision of Patusan and Africa, this view of Russia describes a homogenous space – one empty of distinguishing demarcations.

It is one thing to perceive the open ocean as homogenous because it truly lacks spatial demarcations, but perceiving Patusan, Africa, Russia, or any other non-Western space as homogenous invokes a different kind of perceptual process. The homogeneity that Marlow presents in Patusan and Africa and the teacher of languages presents in Russia is, of course, artificial not actual. In reality, the landscape of Patusan consists of a multiplicity of diversity, just as Africa’s coast is never the same but instead one of infinite variety, and Russia’s expanse encompasses innumerable individual objects and entities. Marlow, though, is accustomed to the heterogeneous space of the West (as is the teacher of languages), divided by its walls, buildings, bridges, fences, cultivated fields – and especially by its sound and activity. For Marlow and the teacher of languages (in his interpretation of Razumov’s perception), the wilderness of Patusan, the coast of Africa, and the expanse of Russia appear homogenous and empty because they are devoid of the familiarity of the West.

Marlow and other Western characters escalate this perception of the spatial homogeneity of the non-West when they go on to depict such spaces in terms of blankness. The captain in “The Secret Sharer,” for instance, refers to “the blank land of Cochin-China” (SS 37). The most striking instance of blankness, however, appears early in *Heart of Darkness*. While walking the streets of London in search of a job, Marlow notices a map in a shop and remembers that as a boy he would muse over their empty spaces: "At that time there were many blank spaces on the earth, and when I saw one that looked particularly inviting on a map (but they all look that) I would put my finger on it and say, 'When I grow up I will go there.' ... But there was one yet [the Congo] – the biggest, the most blank, so to speak– that I had a hankering after" (HD 56).[1] Margaret Cezair-Thompson has noted, "The map in which Africa is a 'blank' space for Marlow, one he has a 'hankering' for, and the later one 'filled' with rivers and names, are not dissimilar in terms of the prevailing imperialist conception of Africa as a kind of *tabula rasa* upon which Westerners could inscribe their adventures and conquests" (172).[2] Given how little was known about central Africa, this description of the Congo as a blank space becomes representative of the disconnect between the Western characters' perception of non-Western space as homogenous and blank and the actual diversity and fullness embodied in such spaces. While the Westerners perceive the non-West as blank, without demarcations, they do so because what they see does not resemble what they see in Western space. The Congo, for example, is silent and blank and homogenous to them because it had yet to be explored and because what they did know of it did not resemble familiar Western space. The Congo is thus a space of silence, blankness, and homogeneity, and in their minds as far opposed to the fullness and heterogeneity of the West as it was possible to conceive. Nevertheless, the demarcations between Western space and the space of Russia, the Congo, the East, and even the open ocean eventually break down, and this erasure evolves through the characters' transformative encounters with non-Western space.

[1] Compare Conrad's own experience as he relates it in *A Personal Record*: "It was in 1868, when nine years old or thereabouts, that while looking at a map of Africa of the time and putting my finger on the blank space then representing the unsolved mystery of that continent, I said to myself, with absolute assurance and an amazing audacity which are no longer in my character now: 'When I grow up I shall go *there*'. ... Yes. I did go there: *there* being the region of Stanley Falls, which in '68 was the blankest of blank spaces on the earth's figured surface" (PR 26; emphasis in the original). See also "Geography and Some Explorers" (GSE 14).

[2] Russell West suggests that in Conrad's "Up-river Notebook" "colonial desire or intention works to consume and then annihilate the content of indigenous space altogether" (123).

These encounters are first signaled by the silence associated with the non-West, because this silence is not meant merely to contrast with the sound of Western space; nor is it merely the ontological state of the non-West. Instead, silence is infused with significance. In many of Conrad's works, this significance is more implicit than explicit and only becomes apparent as characters conclude their transformational journeys. For example, Marlow remarks of the officers in the *Patna* lifeboat, "A silence of the sea, of the sky, merged into one indefinite immensity still as death around these saved, palpitating lives" (LJ 128). Again more implicit than explicit, the narrator of "Karain" remarks that Karain's land "went on stealthily with a troubling effect of solitude" (K 14), and the captain in *The Shadow-Line* refers to the sea's "barrier of awful stillness" (SL 127). These descriptions of silent space ("still as death," "troubling," "awful") suggests that the silence affects these characters.

At other times, though, Conrad makes clear the profound significance silent space has on his characters. For instance, the captain in "The Secret Sharer" says of his ship:

> She floated at the starting-point of a long journey, very still in an immense stillness, the shadows of her spars flung far to the eastward by the setting sun. … There was not a sound in her. … In this breathless pause at the threshold of a long passage we seemed to be measuring our fitness for a long and arduous enterprise, the appointed task of both our existences to be carried out. (SS 8)

Here, the captain links the silence of the sea to the long passage that will measure their existences. Similarly, Mrs. Travers assesses non-Western space when she confesses, "The light, the silence, the mysterious emptiness of this place have suddenly affected my imagination" (R 255). *Victory* augments this effect when the narrator suggests that Heyst "was influenced by the genius of the locality, which was certainly that of silence" (V 141). For Heyst, Mrs. Travers, and the captain of "The Secret Sharer," silence affects them, causing the captain and Mrs. Travers to recognize how the silence of the Eastern space they encounter affects their immediate actions, and, in Heyst's case, going so far as to permanently alter how he responds to the world.

Even more striking, Marlow reveals that for Jim when "suddenly the steam ceased blowing off" from the *Patna*'s engine as the ship traversed the Indian Ocean, "the silence at once became intolerably oppressive" (LJ

105). In this scene, the silence does not merely influence Jim but actually oppresses him. Analogously, near the close of "An Outpost of Progress," the traders experience "the great silence of the surrounding wilderness," which begins "interfering with their hearts" (OP 92). The silence affects Kayerts more than Carlier, and later, as Kayerts sits in a state of silence, he comes to reassess his "old thoughts, convictions" (OP 97). In a matching manner, Marlow suggests of the Congo that "this strange world of plants, and water, and silence ... did not in the least resemble a peace. It was the stillness of an implacable force brooding over an inscrutable intention" (HD 91). He similarly states that "the high stillness of primeval forest was before my eyes" and follows with "I could see through a sombre gap glittering, glittering, as it [the river] flowed broadly by without a murmur. All this was great, expectant, mute. ... I wondered whether the stillness on the face of the immensity looking at us two were meant as an appeal or as a menace. ... I felt how big, how confoundedly big, was that thing that couldn't talk" (HD 82). Marlow concludes that "the silence of the land went home to one's very heart" (HD 82). Jennifer A. Janachek remarks, Marlow "finds the soundless void so powerful that it becomes almost deafening" (22), and Anne McClintock contends that "the landscape reveals its power to invade and to engulf the mind" (49). The space of Africa is silent for Marlow, as it is for Kayerts and Carlier, but it is also ominous, not inherently so but perceived as such, and so much so that it penetrates their being and affects how they will experience the world thereafter.

The most poignant example of the effect of spatial silence occurs in *Nostromo* when Decoud endures a silence he equates with the uninhabited island of the Great Isabel. After reaching this deserted island, "Decoud found himself solitary on the beach like a man in a dream. A sudden desire to hear a human voice once more seized upon his heart" (N 217). Later, he experiences "a day of absolute silence – the first he had known in his life. And he had not slept a wink" (N 356). Like Marlow, Jim, Kayerts, and Carlier, who are emotionally affected by silent space, the silent space of the Great Isabel, a space removed from all traces of the West,[3] so debilitates Decoud that he "slept not a wink, later comes to question his existence,"

[3]Although *Nostromo* is set in South America, Conrad's European characters regularly experience the space they encounter as non-Western. For example, the chairman of the railway "utterly lost touch with the feeling of European life on the background of his exotic surroundings" (N 31). Compare also Decoud's reaction to the Costaguana he perceives when he juxtaposes it against his Parisian experience (*e.g.*, N 167).

and it eventually changes the course of his life (N 359). Ultimately, this silence will profoundly change Kayerts, Marlow, Decoud, and numerous other characters because, as they encounter non-Western space, silence often emerges as one of the primary signals of their questioning the foundations of Western space, ultimately causing them to experience an existential crisis.

These crises occur as they traverse their transformational travels. These metamorphic events, these epiphanies, vary from character to character, both in kind and intensity. For some, they merely gain greater experience and sometimes even success, while for others the experience is so significant that they come to question all that they had previously held to be true. The commonality among these existential journeys, however, is that although they are all signaled by silence, for so many of them, the crucial component of the journey is their encounter with the non-West. The gunrunners in "Karain," the captains in *The Shadow-Line* and "The Secret Sharer," Jim in *Lord Jim*, Lingard in *The Rescue*, Falk in *Falk*, Heyst in *Victory*, Decoud in *Nostromo*, Kayerts in "An Outpost of Progress," and Marlow in "Youth," *Heart of Darkness*, and *Lord Jim* all make transformative journeys through their engagement with non-Western space. For some, their encounter with the non-West alone brings about their transformation; for others, this encounter combines with other significant circumstances to bring about their metamorphosis.

For yet others, the encounter with non-Western space ought to result in a tranformative experience but does not – to the detriment of the individual. A collection of Conrad's characters present natures entirely impervious to their encounter with the non-West. The captain of the *Patna* and its chief engineer in *Lord Jim*, along with Mr. Travers and Mr. Shaw in *The Rescue* are representative instances. Each betrays strong racial bias against the non-Western world, a bias that never alters and that prevents them from ever engaging with the non-Western world in a meaningful manner. The captain of the *Patna* scans the Muslim pilgrims as they file onto the *Patna* and dismisses them: "Look at dese cattle" (LJ 47), effectually dehumanizing the passengers. Similarly, during the *Patna* emergency, the chief engineer tries to fell Jim with a blow because, as he tells him, "I thought you were one of them niggers [Muslim passengers]" (LJ 109). Later, both characters are quite content to abandon ship and leave the Muslims to drown. Whether they would have been equally cavalier about abandoning a ship full of Westerners is impossible to know, although they are loathe to leave George behind and even dangerously delay (they believe) pushing off in the lifeboat, calling for George to join them (LJ 125). They only leave when Jim, whom they mistake for George, leaps into the lifeboat. In any case, given their cultural biases, they certainly have no qualms concerning the collection of "cattle" they left behind.

Mr. Travers and Mr. Shaw, Lingard's first mate, behave similarly. Travers routinely reveals his racial biases. He refers, for example, to "the duty to civilize" non-Westerners (R 147) and philosophizes, "And if the inferior race must perish, it is a gain, a step toward the perfecting of society which is the aim of progress" (R 148). Travers welcomes the extermination of "the inferior race" in the service of "progress." Betraying analogous views, Mr. Shaw says of a potential conflict with indigenous people that when it "came to a difference with niggers of some kind – they had to be taught manners and reason" (R 189). Even more damning, when Shaw discovers Hassim and Immada aboard the *Lightning*, he fumes, "Niggers. In the cuddy! In the cuddy! … I can't have it. … Damme! I've too much respect for myself. … Out you go!" (R 239). Here, Shaw's racial bias extends so far as refusing even to occupy the same space as non-Westerners. Ironically, Hassim and Immada actually show themselves to be better human beings than Shaw, despite his belief in the stature of his Western heritage.

Conrad presents the captain and chief engineer of the *Patna*, along with Travers and Shaw, as static individuals who reflect no evolution of character during the course of their respective narratives. None experiences a transformation through his encounter with the non-West. Lingard and Travers eventually even swap first mates, a situation especially amenable to Shaw, who will now serve Travers, who shares his biases, rather than Lingard, who respects and engages with indigenous individuals. The biases of the *Patna*'s captain and chief engineer, and of Travers and Shaw completely contrast with that of Jim, who refers to the people of Patusan as his own people (LJ 303, 342) and Lingard, who recognizes the dignity of Hassim and Immada, a dignity absent from the captain, chief engineer, Travers, and Shaw. These characters could have responded to the non-West as do Jim and Lingard. They could have experienced a transformation for the better, enlarging themselves and gaining from their encounter with the space of the non-West. Instead, they remain the narrow-minded, unpleasant people they were when the reader first met them.

Edith Travers experiences perhaps the most usual transformation, one that could have ended in success. Her encounter with non-Western space temporarily causes her to conceive of the world completely counter to how she had previously:

> In a few hours of life she had been torn away from all her certitudes, flung into a world of improbabilities. This thought instead of augmenting her distress seemed to soothe her. What she experienced was not doubt and it was not fear. It was something else. … And all this … was taking place outside the limits of her life which remained encircled by an impenetrable darkness and by an impenetrable silence. … The darkness enfolded her like the enervating caress of a sombre universe. It was gentle and destructive. Its languor seduced her soul into surrender. Nothing existed and even all her memories vanished into space. She was content that nothing should exist. (R 244-45)

In contrast to her husband and Mr. Shaw, Edith Travers transcends Western cultural biases and aligns herself with Lingard's perception of the non-West. She experiences a significant metamorphosis that bodes for an entirely new way of engaging with the world – and for a time it does. However, unlike so many other Conrad characters who experience a transformative epiphany, Edith's transformation is only transient. Her ties to the West are too strong, and her transformative experience fails to be sufficient to abandon permanently the cultural barriers between the West and the non-West. Ultimately, she is unable to arrive at an equivalence between Western and non-Western space, the place where so many other characters' transformative travels terminate.

In contrast to Mr. Travers, Mr. Shaw, the *Patna*'s captain and its chief engineer, and even in contrast to Edith Travers, Lingard and Jim, despite their ultimate failures, achieve some success through their engagement with non-Western space. Lingard fails to restore Hassim to his rule, and Hassim and Immada lose their lives during the failed plan, but the disaster develops primarily through circumstances outside his actions. Unlike Travers and Shaw, Lingard betrays no cultural bias toward the non-West. In fact, he freely interacts with this world, and his actions toward Hassim and Immada show his great sacrifice for them. In short, he broadens his vision of the world through his interactions with the non-West. His failure results in part from circumstances beyond his control (Mr. Travers' arrogance and Mrs. Travers refusing to deliver the ring to Lingard) but also partly from his own failing. His decision to prioritize the fate of the Travers vessel and passengers directly results in the final disaster. Although to a lesser degree than Edith Travers, Lingard nevertheless allows his cultural loyalty (and his attraction to Edith) to complicate the delicate balance he had achieved between the suspicious parties accumulated to bring about

Hassim's return to power. In the end, he subtly prioritizes his cultural connections to the West over his connections to the East.

Jim's fate differs. Jim's success is inexorably tied to his engagement with Patusan's non-Western space. There, he shows himself to be all he had imagined himself to be when he leads the stunningly successful attack on Sherif Ali and his followers and frees the local population from Ali's oppression. Perhaps no greater case exists in Conrad's canon of a character achieving success through an encounter with the non-West. Like Lingard, Jim succeeds largely through his ability to abandon cultural bias and accept the local people as his own people, even taking his mate from among them. Unfortunately, like Lingard and Edith, Jim's ultimate inability to free himself fully from Western cultural ties proves to be his undoing. To be sure, the chance event of Gentleman Brown's arrival in Patusan (like the stranding of the Travers vessel in *The Rescue*) is a contributing factor to Jim's failure, but he finally fails because he allows Brown to appeal to their shared Western values (even though Brown eschews such values). Brown thereby manipulates Jim so that the novel ends in tragedy. Had Jim been able to leave his cultural ties behind and entirely embrace the non-Western world where he had so succeeded, had he thrown his support behind the plan that Jewel, Dain Waris, and Doramin had developed for ridding the land of Brown and his bandits rather than allowing Brown's cynical appeal to Western fair play to sway him (LJ 345), Brown could not have effected the disaster that results in Jim's demise.

Willems in *An Outcast of the Islands* and Almayer in *Almayer's Folly*, however, are the most dramatic instances of opportunities missed for a positive transformative experience through an encounter with the non-West. Willems's persistent belief in his racial superiority ultimately leads to tragedy. After he begins his affair with Aïssa, Willems can never abandon his feeling that he has defiled himself thereby, and when Lingard determines to leave Willems in Sambir because of his betrayal, Willems cries, "Take that woman {Aïssa] away – she is sin" (OI 215). Aïssa is sin not because she represents Willems's adultery nor because she acts sinfully but because she is not white. Willems's eventual decision to abandon Aïssa, solely because of her heritage, leads directly to his death.

Almayer's case is even more tragic. As noted previously, he maintains throughout his feelings of racial superiority to the non-Westerners with whom he interacts, Almayer's attitude appears most dramatically when he rejects Nina for choosing her non-Western heritage over her Western heritage: "In the utter wreck of his affections and of all his feelings, in the chaotic disorder of his thoughts, above the confused sensation of physical pain that wrapped him up in a sting as of a whiplash curling round him from his shoulders down to his feet," and he tells her, " I have no daughter" (AF 151-52). Almayer reasons: "That was his idea of his duty to himself – to his race – to his respectable connections; to the whole universe unsettled and shaken by this frightful catastrophe of his life" (AF 152). To his credit, Almayer hesitates before embarking on such a drastic determination: "And yet he was afraid. She had been all in all to him. What if he should let the memory of his love for her weaken the sense of his dignity? She was a remarkable woman; he could see that; all the latent greatness of his nature – in which he honestly believed – had been transfused into that slight, girlish figure. Great things could be done!" Almayer even goes so far as to reconsider his resolution: "What if he should suddenly take her to his heart, forget his shame, and pain, and anger, and – follow her! What if he changed his heart if not his skin and made her life easier between the two loves that would guard her from any mischance! His heart yearned for her." Sadly, despite the pull of love for Nina, Almayer cannot bring himself to follow through on his heart's greatest longing. When he begins to ask himself whether he can choose Nina, he cannot even complete the mental question: "What if he should say that his love for her was greater than …" and instead exclaims: "I will never forgive you, Nina!" (AF 152) and "If you were to come back to me now, the memory of this night would poison all my life" (AF 145). When confronted with this extreme existential crisis, one where he must choose between his love for his daughter and his allegiance to his Western heritage, he chooses his heritage. At that critical juncture, Almayer fails to secure his transformative opportunity, and his subsequent physical death (following his descent into addiction and despair) merely outwardly signals his inward death once he determines to buttress the boundaries between East and West. A transformative happiness was possible had he abandoned the narrative of benefit and abandoned the barriers (both physical and metaphorical) between Eastern and Western space. Instead, he sought to erase all trace of Nina and the non-Western space she represented (AF 154), but Almayer succeeded only in erasing himself and any semblance of the West in Sambir.

Among those characters who experience transformative journeys resulting both from their encounter with non-Western space and through other eventful elements is the captain in "The Secret Sharer." His transformative journey arises both from his encounter with non-Western space as well as with Leggatt. The young captain notes, "A mysterious communication was established already between us two – in the face of that silent, darkened tropical sea" (SS 13). The silence of this tropical sea actually incites the "mysterious communication" between the captain and Leggatt, a communication which will transform the existence of both, but particularly that of the young captain, who begins his adventure by feeling that "if all the truth must be told, I was somewhat of a stranger to myself. … I wondered how far I should turn out faithful to that ideal conception of one's own personality every man sets up for himself secretly" (SS 9). Of course, the captain's transformation occurs primarily through the other significant event he encounters: his silent communion with Leggatt, but the true test of his transformative journey begins and ends in the silence of the empty space of the Eastern seas. When he begins the sailing manœuver that brings him ever so close to shore, the sea was silent and still, "with the great shadow [of the shore of Koh-ring] gliding closer, towering higher, without a light, without a sound. Such a hush had fallen on the ship that she might have been a bark of the dead floating in slowly under the very gate of Erebus" (SS 40), and when the captain then succeeds in turning the ship away from shore, "all was so still in the world" (SS 42). The sea and Koh-ring are the silent, empty spaces where the captain, who began his journey doubting himself, ends by exulting that "no one in the world should stand now between us [himself and his ship], throwing a shadow on the way of silent knowledge and mute affection" (SS 42). Once "a stranger to the ship" (SS 9), the captain is now in "perfect communion" with his command (SS 42), certainly through his communion with Leggatt but also through his communion with the space of Koh-ring and the space of the gulf.

For the captain in *The Shadow-Line*, the role of non-Western space and significant events is the reverse of the captain in "The Secret Sharer," but his transformation is not. He, too, ultimately secures success in the Eastern seas. Unlike "The Secret Sharer," though, for the captain in *The Shadow-Line*, his experience with non-Western space is the most significant factor in his transformative ordeal. Day after day, with his ship becalmed, the captain remains in constant contact with the non-Western space of the sea and the island of Koh-ring, which "seemed to be the centre of the fatal circle. It seemed impossible to get away from it. Day after day it remained in sight" (SL 103). His crew's illness (compounded by the lack of quinine) is a significant factor in the captain's plight and his resulting transformation, but these events occur solely within the silent, empty space of the sea and within sight of the silent, empty space of Koh-ring. The captain is removed from the trappings of the West and solely subject to the irrationality of a space he cannot escape. When he finally reaches Singapore and has crossed the shadow-line separating youth from maturity, his transformation is altogether attributable to his three-week contest with non-Western space. As a *bildungsroman*, the narrator's transformation occurs through the enormous trials he is forced to face, as he sails his command from Bangkok to Singapore. When he meets Captain Giles after his ordeal, he himself recognizes his metamorphosis: "Well, I am no longer a youngster" (SL 135). Like the captain of "The Secret Sharer," the captain of *The Shadow-Line* has not come to question the validity of Western values, nor does he despair because of what he has learned, but his transformation, though more modest than that of some of Conrad's characters, would not have been accomplished without his significant struggle with non-Western space.

In contrast to the captains of "The Secret Sharer" and *The Shadow-Line*, Heyst's encounter with the silent, empty space of the non-West is not an affirmation – or rather it is an affirmation that comes too late. Like the captain in "The Secret Sharer," Heyst's transformative journey results more from associated events than it does directly from his encounter with non-Western space, but, divorced from that space, the events that lead to his existential crisis could never have occurred because he could never have been forced out of his father's philosophy to "look on – make no sound" (V 136). This view of the world is borne out of the materialism and positivism of the West, out of the suspicion of anything that cannot be quantified. As Heyst insists, "Facts. There's nothing worth knowing but facts. Hard facts! Facts alone" (V 6). In fact, following his assertion. Heyst is given the nickname "Hard Facts" (V 6). This philosophy thoroughly encapsulates the dominant positivist philosophical trend of the time that sought certainty solely in that which could be quantified.

Heyst's encounter with non-Western space and particularly with Lena causes him to reassess his entire Western philosophy of existence. Rather than the stoic outlook on life that begins Heyst's journey, he later laments, "Ah, Davidson, woe to the man whose heart has not learned while young to hope, to love – and to put its trust in life!" (V 320). Recognizing too late his missed moment for a more meaningful existence, Heyst no longer has confidence in his Western ideas and so despairs that he takes his own life. To be sure, the proximate cause for Heyst's altered attitude is his lost chance to have embraced a meaning-filled life with Lena (and with humanity in general), but this epiphany's remote cause is a non-Western space where Western philosophy has broken down and exposed its lack of power to provide a productive process for existence.

Marlow's transformative journey in "Youth" is the most unusual because the same silent space of the non-West incites a life-altering experience in both Marlow the character and Marlow the narrator. Unlike so many other Conrad characters who experience life-altering experiences that create existential crises, Marlow the character experiences a different kind of transformational journey. Marlow the character has romanticized the East to the point that he "can never forget [his first view of the East]. It was impalpable and enslaving, like a charm, like a whispered promise of mysterious delight" (Y 95). In his encounter with Eastern space, Marlow the character is forever changed. He has entered an enchanted existence, something about which he previously could only dream, but his dream has become reality, and Bangkok, that "magic" and "blessed name" (Y 19), has become an actual rather than imagined space, so much so that many years later it remains the same for Marlow the narrator such that "all the East is contained in that vision of my youth. It is all in that moment when I opened my young eyes on it"; and even though the silent space of the East remains the vision of Marlow's youth, that vision "is all that is left of it [his first sighting of the East]! Only a moment; a moment of strength, of romance, of glamour – of youth! … A flick of sunshine upon a strange shore, the time to remember," it is now for Marlow the narrator, for whom it has since also become a space of emptiness "the time for a sigh, and – good-by! – Night – Good-by …!" (Y 98), a moment lost in the past that can never be reconstituted. In this way, the space of the non-West at once ushers Marlow the character into the enchanted and long hoped-for world of a dream but at the same time serves as the catalyst that moves Marlow the narrator from life toward death, as Marlow the narrator contrasts his present self with his youthful self. The romanticized youthful view of the East, which encapsulates all his youthful hopes and dreams, has forever slipped into the past, together with that original sighting of the East and all it contained. And despite the pervasive nostalgia for a time and self ever in the past, over and again Marlow the narrator substitutes the hope of distant youth with the reality of approaching death, as images of death proliferate throughout his tale.

In "Karain," both Karain and the Westerners initially perceive a distinct difference between Western and non-Western space. Karain wants to escape Matara's ghost by accompanying the Westerners to their land, whose people "live in unbelief; to whom day is day, and night is night – nothing more, because [they] understand all things seen, and despise all else!" And so he insists, "To your land of unbelief" (K 40). In an ironic reversal, Karain wants to go to the West because he conceives it to be a space of emptiness – empty of everything spiritual and mystical. The Westerners do not dissuade Karain from this view. To the contrary, Hollis murmurs approvingly, "Capital description" (K 41). At this point, strict boundaries persist between the Eastern space of Karain's land and the Western space of the ship. While aboard ship, Karain evades Matara's ghost, and he fears leaving this Western space and returning to his land of non-Western space with Matara's ghost awaiting him there.

By the end of the story, however, the gunrunners are also forced to come to terms with themselves and their world through their encounter with the non-Western world, as each in his own way experiences a transformation through his interaction with this space. The Jubilee six-pence becomes the catalyst for their transformation. Realizing the impracticality of taking Karain with them, the Westerners take a remarkable step, one that reverberates beyond the immediacy of Karain's conundrum. In creating the charm from the six-pence, Hollis denies Western disbelief in Karain's ghost; in effect, he rejects a primary tenet of the narrative of benefit, which sought to dismiss what the West considered ungodly superstition (to be replaced with godly religion). Of course, the gunrunners do not believe in the charm (although they insist to Karain that they do). Nevertheless, they collectively refuse to dissuade Karain from his superstitions and substitute them with Western "truths" (as insisted on by the narrative of benefit). Rather, they reaffirm his belief that Matara's ghost can be banished by a coin. In this act, Hollis removes a considerable boundary between Western and non-Western space. Through this ceremony, the barrier between Karain's non-Western land and the Western enclave of the ship has dissipated, and the two spaces have now merged. In taking this ultimate symbol of the West (an emblem of the British empire and marker of British money) and transforming it into an Eastern charm, Eastern and Western space merge at the locus of the space of the ship because the charm exists now in both Eastern and Western worlds.

Hollis's transformation is perhaps the most straightforward. He does not believe Karain's tale, but he shows significant sympathy for him and gives him "something that I shall really miss" (K 45), creating an elaborate ritual to invoke unseen powers to invest unseen protection in a Jubilee six-pence, an object which was once an image of the West but is now an image of both the West and the non-West. The moment the charm hangs around Karain's neck, the six-pence loses its material meaning, although it retains its Western origins. It is no longer currency to be spent but a charm to subdue spirits (as did Karain's old sword-bearer). Like the six-pence, Hollis, also, has been changed. He has reinforced Karain's immaterial world and has broken with the pervasive power of Western materialism, a materialism that had become for so many of the time the only certainty in the aftermath of Darwin, Spencer, Comte, Huxley, and others. Hollis has become an inextricable and material part of Karain's immaterial world.

The unnamed narrator's transformation comes differently. Not only Karain's experience itself but the narrator's relating it lead to his transformation. Mark Conroy remarks that "the frame narrator is subject to the same self-consciousness, the same anxiety, as Karain is" (9). The narrator is "surprised and moved" by Karain's tale (K 38), but he quickly re-erects the borders between Western and non-Western space when he hears the Greenwich time of the ship's chronometers, which, as noted earlier, provide him with "protection and a relief" (K 38). Much like Heyst, he also insists on the ascendency of the material world and tries to convince Jackson of the same when he shows him the bustle of the London Strand (K 48), but as Richard Ambrosini suggests, the narrator is nevertheless "changed by his experience in the Archipelago," and his "enlarged vision" is "disconnected from the common perception of reality. His very past sets him apart from his audience"; his "basic idiosyncrasy is an unresolved contradiction between Western disbelief and Eastern illusion" (74). Furthermore, the narrator's experience in the East allows him to recognize the immateriality of Western materiality. This recognition is apparent when he classifies the various icons from Hollis's leather box, "a couple of reels of cotton, a packet of needles, a bit of silk ribbon, dark blue; a cabinet photograph" and "a lot of various small objects, a bunch of flowers, a narrow white glove with many buttons, a slim packet of letters carefully tied up," as "Amulets of white men! Charms and talismans! Charms that keep them straight, that drive them crooked, that have the power to make a young man sigh, an old man smile. Potent things that procure dreams of joy, thoughts of regret; that soften hard hearts, and can temper a soft one to the hardness of steel. Gifts of heaven – things of earth" (K 43). Classification is a singularly scientific endeavor, one tightly tied to Western ideas of the time concerning the ascendency of science and the material world to supply certainty. Ironically, however, the narrator marshals this practice of materiality to come to immaterial conclusions. In other words, the narrator's final determination of the purpose of these artifacts from Hollis's leather box is not as practical objects of materiality but impractical ones of spirituality: "amulets", "charms," and "talismans." As such, the narrator too no longer sees the world the West posits, where "day is day, and night is night – nothing more" (K 40). Rather, he recognizes an immaterial aura enveloping his material Western world.

Jackson most obviously traverses a transformative space, but the role of non-Western space in Jackson's transformative travels transpires differently. For him, the barriers between Western and non-Western space are never entirely re-established after Karain's tale, and Jackson actually comes to question the ascendency of the Western world when (despite the narrator forcing him to confront the material immediacy of the London Strand) he acknowledges the reality of this London scene but nevertheless no longer finds it as real "as … as the other thing … say, Karain's story" (K 49). Whether Jackson's "feeling that the world of Karain is more real than London" (Hawthorn 78), or whether he merely wonders whether Karain's experience is true, Jackson reveals his blurring the borders between Western and non-Western space. Merely entertaining the possibility of the reality of Karain's story of haunting while standing at the epicenter of Western materiality – with all its suspicion of anything it cannot quantify – produces a metaphorical blending of the two spheres, and his musings on a world of spirits emerging in the full face of the sound-filled activity of the West suggests that while he may not have abandoned his Western values, the boundaries between Western and non-Western space are for him far more permeable than they once were – before he traveled to the East and encountered Karain's world. Again, like the Jubilee six-pence, the ultimate symbol of Western materialism, Jackson has been altered. For him, too, the West is no longer a place where Western materialism rules alone. It is no longer a "land of unbelief, where the dead do not speak" (K 40). It has become instead a land where Matara's specter can indeed speak.

Somewhat similar to Jackson, Mr. Burns in *The Shadow-Line* flouts the materiality of the West when he insists on the supernatural hold the ship's former captain has over their vessel. Burns blames the former captain for the ship's lying in the doldrums, unable to make headway toward their destination. When the former captain died, he was buried at sea at latitude 8° 20′, and Burns believes that their lack of progress "was the fault of the 'old man' – the late captain – ambushed down there under the sea with some evil intention" (SL 97; see also 101). Burns is convinced that "the great thing is to get the ship past 8° 20′ of latitude" and insists that "once she's past that we're all right" (SL 104). The young captain rejects this notion and at first merely humors Mr. Burns. Later, the captain echoes Western materiality when he loses patience and exclaims, "Don't you think, Mr. Burns, it's about time you dropped all that nonsense?" (SL 104), but Burns ignores the rebuke and merely muses on his former captain: "Not surprised … find … play us some beastly trick yet. …" (SL 104). Burns believes that by laughing in the face of the dead captain, they can escape his hold over them and urges the crew, "Well, then – laugh! Laugh – I tell you. Now then – all together. One, two, three – laugh!" (SL 127). Whether Mr. Burns has always held such anti-material views, the narrative does not disclose, but his encounter with the non-Western space of the Eastern seas, particularly the specific spatial location of latitude 8° 20′ north, silences any Western materiality he might have heard, and he wholly gives himself over to a very different view of the world, a view achieved through engaging with this space of the East.

Late in the novel, the young captain seems to suggest a striking reassessment of his prior skepticism: "By the exorcising virtue of Mr. Burns' awful laugh, the malicious spectre had been laid, the evil spell broken, the curse removed. We were now in the hands of a kind and energetic Providence. It was rushing us on…" (SL 130). The narrator may or may not have been converted to Mr. Burns's non-material view of the situation and may only be speaking ironically, but regardless he no longer dismisses out of hand the idea of the former captain's hold over his vessel, because the change in their fortunes from painfully languishing in the doldrums to suddenly speeding along at the behest of a runaway wind is truly remarkable – in fact miraculous. Converted or not, the young captain's statement that "the malicious spectre had been laid, the evil spell broken, the curse removed" results from his encounter with this non-Western space. As a *bildungsroman* where the narrator crosses from youth to maturity, his encounter with the silent emptiness of the Gulf of Siam also seems to have caused him, like the narrator of "Karain," at least momentarily to reassess his confidence that Western materiality alone can explain the phenomena of the universe. Perhaps for him, too, the world is not merely a world where "day is day, and night is night – nothing more" (K 40).

Falk's transformative journey varies in yet another manner from that of these other characters. Adrift on the open ocean, Falk experiences "the sea ruled by iron necessity, its spectral band swayed by terror and hope, its mute and unhearing heaven" (F 192). Pushed to the extremes of hunger in the silent and empty Southern Ocean, Falk violates one of the most inviolable Western taboos when he eats his dead companions, cannibalism being perhaps the most impermeable of barriers between Western space and non-Western space. For Westerners, cannibalism only occurs in non-Western space and was for Westerners one of the most distinctive markers of the non-West, a primary target of the narrative of benefit. Naturally, the necessity to survive drives Falk to this act, but many Westerners find such justification nevertheless unacceptable, and Falk thus conceals his ordeal from all and only discloses his breach of taboo because he feels he must disclose his past to any prospective spouse. While petitioning Hermann for his niece's hand, Falk informs him of his cannibalism. Hermann understands that extreme exigencies drove Falk to that act, but such a breach of Western values is just too much for him:

> Hermann suddenly put both his hands up with a jerk. The embroidered calotte fell, and, in the twinkling of an eye, he had rumpled his hair all ends up in a most extravagant manner. In this state he strove to speak; with every effort his eyes seemed to start further out of their sockets; his head looked like a mop. He choked, gasped, swallowed, and managed to shriek out the one word, "Beast!" (F 179)

Despite Falk's effort to explain himself, Hermann asks him "how dared he to come and tell him this" and "whether he did think there was anywhere on earth a woman abandoned enough to mate with such a monster" (F 180). Hermann never reconciles to Falk's cannibalism and only relents and gives his consent to marry his niece because she wants to marry Falk and would be of no use as a family helper in her state of disappointment had Hermann barred the match. In this case, Falk's transformative experience comes about because of physical necessity, but in eating the dead crew members, Falk erases one of the most rigid boundaries between Western and non-Western spaces, and in the non-Western space of the Southern Ocean, Falk and his fellow crew members (who also engaged in cannibalism) transform the Western space aboard the *Borgmester Dahl* into non-Western space where cannibalism is permitted. Hermann and other like-minded Westerners who strictly hold to Western values, cannot view Falk as a Westerner but only as a "Beast!" (F 179).

Among the characters who complete transformative journeys, such as Falk, the gunrunners, or the captain in *The Shadow-Line*, they in some way either violate Western values or otherwise remove barriers between Western and non-Western space. Nevertheless, all in some way at least temporarily traduce a direct correlation between the empty space of the non-West and the full space of the West. In other words, they interrogate the barriers Westerners erect between Western and non-Western space. There are, however, other characters who not only remove such barriers but who come to see both Western and non-Western spaces as spaces of silence and emptiness, and once they arrive at this terminus to their transformative travels, they are then confronted with a universe of nothingness. As Irving Howe once noted, "Long before Hemingway began to look for a clean well-lighted place, Conrad knew the meaning of *nada*" (81). For characters who perceive the space around them, Western and non-Western, as spaces of absence, their metamorphic journeys end at a space where they must entirely reassess the world as they had previously conceived it and determine how to confront a universe of absence.

Decoud is one such individual, and he presents the most direct link between the silence and absence of non-Western space and a life-altering and, most poignantly in his case, life-ending expedition of existential crisis. When he first appears, he is famously skeptical, but his skepticism does not reach the degree of erasing the boundaries between Western and non-Western space or rejecting Western values as being without inherent truth. In fact, his skeptical critique of Costaguana politics arises precisely from an acceptance of Western values. While looking at the "narrow openings like loopholes for windows" at Viola's inn, Decoud writes to his sister that these narrow windows were "probably used in old times for the better defence against the savages, when the persistent barbarism of our native continent did not wear the black coats of politicians, but went about yelling, half-naked, with bows and arrows in its hands" (N 167). Decoud's disdain for local politics is based upon his acceptance of a Western view of morals in representative governments while seeing a concurrent lack of such in Costaguana's history.

Yael Levin argues that Nostromo's presence aboard the lighter spiriting away the shipment of silver during the Sulaco secession allows Decoud "to erect boundaries between himself and the world, to separate himself from a chaos wherein all separations have been canceled out into an undifferentiated void where 'Even his hand held before his face did not exist for his eyes' [N 189]" (140), but the same is true of Nostromo's presence on the Great Isabel – until Nostromo leaves. Once alone on this uninhabited island, Decoud is isolated from the Western influence of Sulaco and his Paris upbringing, and, in the silent, empty space of this island, ensconced in the middle of a gulf that is also described as both silent and empty (*e.g.*,

N 7, 194, 211, 298, 352), Decoud is unable to "erect boundaries between himself and the world" and instead experiences his transformative journey.

As soon as Nostromo sails away, Decoud begins to experience the silence of this empty space. He "was oppressed by a bizarre sense of unreality affecting the very ground upon which he walked" (N 218). At first, it may seem that Decoud despairs because he believes that the secession has failed when Nostromo does not return right away: "Nostromo was dead. Everything had failed ignominiously. He no longer dared to think of Antonia. She had not survived" (N 357), and Decoud knows that "Montero, should he be successful, would get even with [him] in the only way such a brute can get even with a man of intelligence who condescends to call him a *gran bestia* three times a week" (N 131). Decoud's fear of a failed secession, though, only contributes toward his descent to despair. Instead, day upon day confronting this silent, empty space, Decoud comes to perceive it, a space removed from the trappings of the West, as a space of absence and finally comes to "behold the universe as a succession of incomprehensible images" (N 357). Even if Antonia, his beloved, has survived, "he could not face her" because "all exertion seemed senseless" (N 357). In this silent space, Decoud's skepticism has shifted. Previously, his skepticism was based on the gap between Decoud's Western values and the reality he encountered in Costaguana, but after confronting the space of the Great Isabel and the Golfo Placido enveloping it, "Decoud caught himself entertaining a doubt of his own individuality" and "lost all belief in the reality of his action past and to come" (N 357). He grows convinced of the "utter uselessness of all effort" (N 358) and finally "believed in nothing" (N 359).

Once he enters this life-changing existence, "having gone mad with protracted silence" (Fogel 128), his transformative experience evolves from life-changing to life-ending:

> The solitude [of the Great Isabel] appeared like a great void, and the silence of the gulf like a tense, thin cord to which he hung suspended by both hands, without fear, without surprise, without any sort of emotion whatever. Only towards the evening, in the comparative relief of coolness, he began to wish that this cord would snap. ... And that would be the end of him. He contemplated that eventuality with pleasure, because he dreaded the sleepless nights in which the silence, remaining unbroken in the shape of a cord to which he hung with both hands, vibrated with senseless phrases, always the same but utterly incomprehensible. (N 357-58)

Perceiving a universe of silent absence, "a succession of incomprehensivle images" (N 396), Decoud no longer has "faith in himself and others," and "the truth was that he died from solitude" (N 356). Fixed in his newly acquired conviction of a universe of nothingness, Decoud rows out to the silent, blankness of the gulf and shoots himself. The narrator seals Decoud's perception when noting that Decoud's body fell overboard and disappeared "without a trace, swallowed up in the immense indifference of things" (N 359). Such a universe of absence cannot be other than indifferent to Decoud's psychological suffering and troubling tragedy.

Decoud had previously experienced a heterogeneous world, the Western world he inhabited, one where, despite his skeptical perception, meaning and distinctions could be discovered, especially in his love for Antonia, but at the close of his life, all has disappeared and become an absolute absence. By having Decoud take his life not on the island but out in the gulf (though in sight of the empty island space), Conrad once again emphasizes a homogenous empty space, one devoid of demarcations. As noted earlier, the sea is the perfect metaphor for homogenous emptiness, with every inch looking exactly like every other inch, and the Golfo Placido takes this homogeneity a step further, earning its name because it exhibits less movement than a typical body of water such that even distinction between waves is absent, its surface being an unbroken sheet of static space.[4]

Just before he takes his life, Decoud looks at the empty gulf, as it "burst into a glitter all around the boat"; despite its beauty, "in this glory of merciless solitude the silence appeared again before him, stretched taut like a dark, thin string" (N 359). The universe had become for him a great and silent void, a void where he can no longer exist. Surrounded by the "merciless solitude" (N 359) of the empty gulf and silent island, Decoud comes to question the Western values he had previously accepted and correspondingly comes to question the boundaries between Western and non-Western space. As he ponders the Western world he left behind in light of the non-Western world he experiences of the Golfo Placido and the Great Isabel, he comes more and more to see the Western world as illusory and devoid of meaning or value, eventually arriving at the conviction that all space, Western and non-Western, is a silent and empty absence.

Like Decoud, Kayerts in "An Outpost of Progress" and Marlow in *Heart of Darkness* experience particularly poignant transformative

[4] The gulf's placidness is the reason that sailing ships could not navigate it, and the region remained isolated until the era of steam ships (N 5).

journeys through their contact with non-Western space, journeys that cause them to question all that they had previously believed. Perhaps because these tales take place in the Congo, the space of Conrad's own transformative journey where he believed that he transformed from an instinctive animal to a sentient human being (Jean-Aubry 1: 141; Garnett 8), Kayerts and Marlow most strikingly demonstrate the consequences of this journey within and its arrival at absolute absence.

As do so many of Conrad characters, Kayerts and Marlow begin their journeys by perceiving distinct differences between Western and non-Western space, but they end by dismissing those differences. Conrad complicates this process by employing the doubling mechanism noted earlier, a narrative of immediacy that highlights the distinction between what the narrator knows and what the character experiences, thus presenting phenomena from the consciousness of the character rather than from the consciousness of the narrator. At the point that the narrator of "An Outpost of Progress" relates the events of the story to the reader and Marlow narrates his tale to his listeners, Kayerts and Marlow have already suffered through their life-changing Congo ordeal (as had Conrad when he wrote these stories). By this juncture, these characters have come to see the absence of both Western and African space. The narrators already know the conclusion to their characters' existential experience, but they narrate their tales primarily from the characters' perspective of evolutionary development, and in this way, they chronicle their process of discovery (with which Conrad's readers and Marlow's listeners participate). In a sense, the reader of "An Outpost of Progress" and the reader and listener of Marlow's tale accompany the characters on their own existential journeys. The effect of this confluence of the narrators' accumulated experience and the characters' accumulating experience is both a distinguishing and a blurring of boundaries between sound and silence, fullness and emptiness, civilized and savage, West and non-West.

Like the main characters of these chronicles, Conrad's readers (and Marlow's listeners) discover distinctions between boundaries between the West and the non-West that eventually dissolve, resulting in the general negation of distinguishing demarcations that accompanies the negation of spatial demarcations. Just as sonic emptiness is a metonym for spatial emptiness, spatial emptiness is a metonym for metaphysical emptiness, the emptiness of nothingness: the view of a universe without order, without reason, without meaning.

The Western characters in Conrad's African tales perceive African space to be empty, but those same characters (except for Marlow) transform the metaphorical Western spaces they inhabit in Africa into spaces of emptiness, spaces without order, reason, or meaning. Moreover, they transform themselves into creatures without order, reason, or meaning. They and the spaces they inhabit become embodiments of negation.

This focus first emerges in the accouterments of the West. As demonstrated in the preceding chapter, espoused Western morality is absent from these tales. However, this absence is only one facet of the absence of the values through which the West defined itself. These Westerners also abandon the Western values of order and reason. For instance, while traveling down the coast of Africa, Marlow encounters a French man-of-war and assesses, "In the empty immensity of earth, sky, and water, there she was, incomprehensible, firing into a continent. Pop, would go one of the six-inch guns; a small flame would dart and vanish, a little white smoke would disappear, a tiny projectile would give a feeble screech – and nothing happened. Nothing could happen" (HD 65). In this act, not only is this incident of Western politics and society and the narrative of benefit shown to be without effect on the non-Western world, it also linked to an absence of reason. The "objectless blasting" Marlow encounters shortly thereafter is similar: the detonation shakes the ground, and smoke emerges from the cliff, but nothing happens. The cliff is unchanged (HD 67). Again, like the French man-of-war, the civilizing activity lacks sense; nothing happens, and worse, not only does nothing happen (no benefit accrues), but the entire enterprise is devoid of purpose: "They were building a railway. The cliff was not in the way or anything; but this objectless blasting was all the work going on" (HD 67). Marlow himself recognizes the link to the French warship when he says, "Another report from the cliff made me think suddenly of that ship of war I had seen firing into a continent" (HD 68). Like the warship "firing into a continent," the "objectless blasting" is associated with an absence of reason and effect. These actions are also associated with an absence of ethics because when Marlow later sees the chain gang, he connects their plight with both the objectless blasting and "the bursting shells" of the colonizing man-of war (HD 68). Consequently, reason, morals, and effect are absent as these elements of Western presence in Africa merge with African space.

Just as the chain gang betrays a lack of Western morals, so also does the "grove of death." When Marlow tries to avoid the chain gang and its implications of Western absence, he steps into the darkness of the grove, only to discover an even more bleak absence. Marlow says of its inhabitants that "they were nothing earthly now – nothing but black shadows of disease and starvation, lying confusedly in the greenish gloom. … These moribund shapes were free as air – and nearly as thin" (HD 69). Marlow notes one in particular, who "stared at nothing, in an intolerable and appalling manner" and relates, "While I stood horror-struck, one of these creatures rose to his hands and knees" (HD 70). The repetition of negation – from the Africans' near absence of physical substance to the blankness of the one fellow's stare to their unearthly existence – combine to reveal a space of absence which also discloses Western absence in this African setting, Western presence in Africa being the source for the grove of death.

Not only elements of Western presence exhibit absence, but the Westerners themselves are revealed to be vessels of absence In "An Outpost of Progress," Kayerts and Carlier "did nothing, absolutely nothing" (OP 81), and the narrator relates that they "understood nothing, cared for nothing" (OP 82). They come to embody absence. *Heart of Darkness* delineates this process even more dramatically. Marlow first notices this absence when he observes that the officials on his transport vessel traveling to the Congo show no concern when they land soldiers and clerks along the way, some of whom are drowned in the surf, but "nobody seemed particularly to care. They were just flung out there, and on we went" (HD 64). This lack of compassion for the drowned men anticipates the company's chief accountant, who, as we have seen, reflects a similar lack of both compassion and ethics through his unsympathetic attitude toward the dying trader, his wish that the noisy Africans were dead, and his coercing an African woman to do his laundry (HD 71, 72). Along with the absence of ethics the traders exhibit, the brickmaker and the station manager reveal a more general absence. As Marlow rehearses his conversation with the brickmaker, he remarks, "I let him run on, this papier-mâché Mephistopheles, and it seemed to me that if I tried I could poke my forefinger through him, and would find nothing inside but a little loose dirt, maybe" (HD 82). Marlow assesses the station manager similarly:

> He was a common trader from his youth up employed in these parts. – nothing more. He was obeyed, yet he inspired neither love nor fear, nor even respect. … He had no genius for organizing, for initiative, or for order even. … He had no learning, and no intelligence. … He originated nothing. … Perhaps there was nothing within him. (HD 76)

The accumulation of this concatenation of collective absences equates the station manager with the brickmaker: there is nothing within him; he is simply an absence. When the manager complains concerning the many traders who fall ill that "men who come out here should have no entrails" (HD 76), he unwittingly voices a universal absence among the Western traders: that is, to succeed in the Congo they must be hollow.

The most profound example of human absence appears in Kurtz, who exhibits the greatest degree of moral and social absence, eschewing both when pursuing ivory and worship. He employs "no method at all" (HD 125) in collecting ivory because "there was nothing on earth to prevent him killing whom he jolly well pleased" (HD 118). Marlow says, "There was nothing either above or below him, and I knew it. He had kicked himself loose of the earth" (HD 130) and concludes that Kurtz was a "hollow sham" (HD 132) and "hollow at the core" (HD 120). Stephen Ross posits that Kurtz's deathbed declaration, "The horror! The horror!" (HD 134), is actually "a glimpse of the hollowness within himself" (47). Even Kurtz's Intended unwittingly affirms Kurtz's hollowness when she says that "of all his promise, and of all his greatness, of his generous mind, of his noble heart, nothing remains" (HD 141). The intended believes these qualities died with him, but they had left him long before his death, leaving an absence in their stead. These hollow men (the brickmaker, the station manager, Kurtz, and the other Westerns in Africa) do not merely expose an absence of ethics or an absence of sympathy, but they are themselves ontological absences, beings without order, reason, or meaning, providing no benefit to the non-Western world and inhabiting a space (the Western trading stations) that reflects those same negations. Through their encounters with the empty elements of the West that Kayerts and Marlow uncover while in the Congo, both come to perceive the emptiness of the West itself, and this discovery breaks down the spatial barriers between the West and the non-West upon which they initially insist.

From the very opening of *Heart of Darkness*, Conrad begins blurring Western and African spatial boundaries. The frame narrator refers to the "traffic of the great city" (HD 55) and points to the bustle surrounding the Thames (noting even the activity of its historical explorers), thereby equating Western space with activity, sound, and also light (HD 52). As we have seen, the Western world disseminates its light, believing it illuminates the darkness of the non-Western world (the narrative of benefit), but as Robert Hampson contends of this space, "What had seemed fixed and familiar becomes open and indeterminate" (59). This process begins when

Marlow the narrator introduces a counterclaim to the frame narrator's laudatory remarks with the rejoinder that England "has been one of the dark places of the earth" (HD 52).[5] Again, when Marlow looks at the map of Africa in the shop window, he associates the Congo with blankness, but he soon qualifies that appellation, acknowledging, "True, by this time it was not a blank space any more. It had got filled since my boyhood with rivers and lakes and names. It had ceased to be a blank space. … It had become a place of darkness" (HD 56), in other words, "a crucial source of revelation and knowledge" (Acheraïou 40). Marlow the narrator and Marlow the character are both present at this moment. Marlow the character encounters the Congo as a blank space on the map, not as blank as when he was a boy since "rivers and lakes and names" were now present, yet still "the biggest, the most blank" space. At the same time, it can only be Marlow the narrator who describes the Congo as "a place of darkness." Allon White argues that at the opening of *Heart of Darkness* "the darkness is only gloomy: it will intensify to total blackness as the narrative unfolds" (114-15). This transformation evolves as Marlow comes to perceive African space as a "place of darkness," a conclusion arrived at through having completed his existential expedition.

Much has been said about darkness in Conrad's *Heart of Darkness*,[6] but little has been said about its relationship to blankness. Marlow the narrator does not perceive blankness and darkness to be opposites to light and dark but instead as correlatives of homogeneity; the Congo is a blankness and a darkness at the same time because heterogeneity is absent in the homogeneity of both blank and dark spaces. Further emphasizing such homogeneity, David Toop suggests that darkness in Conrad is an "equivalent or manifestation of absolute silence" (196). In such a state of darkness, blankness, and silence, all distinctions are negated, leaving a metaphorical emptiness in their aftermath.[7]

[5] The frame narrator refers to those explorers who had departed on their adventures from the Thames River as "the great knights-errant of the sea" (HD 51) and lauds them: "What greatness had not floated on the ebb of that river into the mystery of an unknown earth! … The dreams of men, the seed of commonwealths, the germs of empires" (HD 52). That the frame narrator voices these sentiments to his companions aboard the *Nellie* is clear when Marlow replies with "you say Knights?" (HD 53).

[6] Several notable examples include Wilfred S. Dowden, J. Hillis Miller (13-67), and Ian Watt (249-53).

[7] Miller sees a similar correlation between white light and darkness, both states negating distinctions (27).

Consequently, when Marlow insists that London was once a dark space (HD 52), he creates a correlative between darkness and blankness, in contrast to the frame narrator's implied distinction between Western and non-Western space as he affirms the narrative of benefit. Designating London as a dark place of the earth is a particularly powerful retort to the frame narrator's praise of England's imperial past (and then present). England was the most powerful nation on earth at the time, in effect the epicenter of the civilized world, with London as England's epicenter and the perceived absolute opposite to the Congo. In associating England with darkness, though, Marlow the narrator dramatically dismantles the perceived barriers between the light of the West and the dark of the non-West.

While recounting his African experience, Marlow will come to reveal the sound and activity and light of the West to be what he will later call "the mere incidents of the surface" (HD 91). Marlow suggests that these "mere incidents of the surface" do not actually alter the Thames from what it was when the Romans first arrived. In other words, the accouterments of civilization surrounding the Thames are simply constructs that have failed to banish the historical Thames from the contemporary Thames. In teasing out this connection, Marlow dismisses the differences between the Thames and the Congo, and, rather than being the opposites upon which the Western world insisted, the Thames and the Congo instead mirror one another when Marlow describes the Thames the Romans encountered in the same language he will later describe the Congo he encountered. In the end, the seemingly "unbridgeable differences between London and Africa" transform "into a revelation of their uncanny resemblance" (Greaney 68).[8] By equating England with darkness, Marlow dismisses the sound, activity, and light that the frame narrator praises, but Marlow also reveals his view of England as a space of absence. When Marlow the narrator initiates his narrative of immediacy and shifts to relating Marlow the character's experience in the Congo, the tale begins with distinctions between Western and African space. It is Marlow the character who initially sees the Congo as a blank space on the map in contradistinction to its un-blank Western spaces; it is Marlow the

[8] Marlow will conclude his tale with a similar correlative when he connects the African woman at the inner station with the Intended: "She put out her arms as if after a retreating figure, stretching them back and with clasped pale hands across the fading and narrow sheen of the window, … and I shall see her, too, a tragic and familiar Shade, resembling in this gesture another one, tragic also, and bedecked with powerless charms, stretching bare brown arms over the glitter of the infernal stream, the stream of darkness" (HD 141-42).

character who describes African space as silent and empty as opposed to Western space's sound and activity. Only gradually (through Marlow the character's transformative travels) do the boundaries between the two spaces dissolve.

Conrad connects African space with silence to reveal its ultimate absence not because the West in contrast embodied for him the truth of an orderly universe but rather because the non-West lacked what Marlow calls elsewhere the "arrangement of small conveniences" that the Western world had created and that allow for the illusion of an orderly universe (LJ 288). Marlow details the role of these "small conveniences" when he reveals his response to hearing Jewel's tale of her mother's death:

> It had the power to drive me out of my conception of existence, out of that shelter each of us makes for himself to creep under in moments of danger, as a tortoise withdraws within its shell. For a moment I had a view of a world that seemed to wear a vast and dismal aspect of disorder, while, in truth, thanks to our unwearied efforts, it is as sunny an arrangement of small conveniences as the mind of man can conceive. But still – it was only a moment: I went back into my shell directly. One *must* – don't you know? – though I seemed to have lost all my words in the chaos of dark thoughts I had contemplated for a second or two beyond the pale. These came back too very soon, for words also belong to the sheltering conception of light and order which is our refuge. (LJ 288; emphasis in original)

In other words, while Conrad does not perceive the Western world as embodying a universe of meaning and order, the "small conveniences," the West's psychological shelters, help provide the appearance of such a universe in order to hide its pervasive emptiness. As Marlow remarks, "When you have to attend to things of that sort, to the mere incidents of the surface, the reality – the reality, I tell you – fades. The inner truth is hidden – luckily, luckily" (HD 91). Mark A. Wollaeger remarks of Marlow's reliance on "mere incidents of the surface," "One needs to shield oneself in work, here defined as part of surface reality, in order to escape from the vague threat of a hidden, second-order reality" (62), a "second-order reality" that is the reality of a universe of absence concealed beneath these "mere incidents." In this way, "mere incidents of the surface" or "small conveniences" conceal the blankness – "luckily."

Established institutions are among these "small conveniences." When Marlow laments that his listeners cannot fully grasp the reality of his

Congo experience, he explains, "This is the worst of trying to tell. … Here you all are, each moored with two good addresses, like a hulk with two anchors, a butcher round one corner, a policeman round another" (HD 108). Marlow sees such externals as moorings that provide one with psychological and cosmological stability and with the illusion that the world is one of recognizable truths – just as Marlow's focus on "mere incidents of the surface" (HD 91) allows him to shelter temporarily from the troubling truths he uncovers in the Congo. Like the "mere incidents of the surface," though, these externals – these anchors – are only respites while they are persistently present. Once gone, what remains is not an ordered and meaningful universe but one the silence speaks: one with neither sense nor substance.

Marlow here echoes the power the streets of London hold for the narrator of "Karain" (K 48-49) in blocking out everything but the immediacy of their reality, but while Marlow's listeners have solid pavement under their feet and are in the presence of policemen and neighbors and the other trappings of civilization, he asks them, "How can [they] imagine what particular region of the first ages a man's untrammelled feet may take him into by the way of solitude – utter solitude without a policeman – by the way of silence – utter silence, where no warning voice of a kind neighbour can be heard whispering of public opinion? (HD 110). Marlow follows by insisting that "these little things make all the great difference" (HD 110). These "little things" – laws, opinions, conventions – provide needed external restraints because Marlow, through embarking on his existential expedition and especially through his engagement with the Congo and with Kurtz (who himself showed "no restraint" (HD 112; see also 120, 130)), has come to recognize that few individuals exhibit internal restraint in the absence of external restraint. Marlow has concluded that these "little things," these external restraints, are mere social contracts and that no transcendental restraints exist – only contingent ones (whether internal or external). In other words, he uncovers an absence of the universe the Western world asserts, a world whose truths have now become for Marlow contingent rather than transcendent, erected only through personal boundaries or social structures.

The narrator of "An Outpost of Progress" also recognizes these "little things," these "small conveniences," these "mere incidents of the surface," calling them instead the "habitual," which he describes as "safe" (OP 79). Conrad contends that Westerners rely on the "habitual" to provide shelter from a knowledge of the nature of the universe and to provide structure and meaning to individual and communal existence, so much so that Westerners are often unaware that the "habitual," these "little things," these "small conveniences," these "mere incidents of the surface" are only psychological shelters and social contracts that make life livable. As the narrator of "An Outpost of Progress" insists:

> Few men realize that their life, the very essence of their character, their capabilities and their audacities, are only the expression of their belief in the safety of their surroundings. The courage, the composure, the confidence; the emotions and principles; every great and every insignificant thought belongs not to the individual but to the crowd: to the crowd that believes blindly in the irresistible force of its institutions and of its morals, in the power of its police and of its opinion. (OP 79)

Only when Westerners are removed from these "little things," when they experience "the negation of the habitual" (OP 79), as the narrator calls it, can they comprehend how much they lean on the "habitual" to provide order, structure, and meaning for their existence while they unwittingly confront an empty universe. In contrast, for Conrad's Westerners, unfamiliar with the non-West, the non-Western world is without the "little things," without the "small conveniences," without the "mere incidents of the surface," without the "habitual" and can thus provide no respite from a universe of absence.

Kayerts and Carlier discover firsthand the consequences of "the negation of the habitual." The two traders' confidence in the narrative of benefit, the Western civilizing mission, eventually wanes because the familiar "force of [the West's] institutions and of its morals" proves to be without force in Africa and instead is unveiled as only the "habitual," the "little things," the "small conveniences," the "mere incidents of the surface." In the wake of their negation, the traders experience "an inarticulate feeling that something from within them was gone, something that worked for their safety, and had kept the wilderness from interfering with their hearts." They find that "the images of home; the memory of people like them, of men that thought and felt as they used to think and feel, receded into distances made indistinct by the glare of unclouded sunshine." These elements of safety disappear, and "out of the great silence of the surrounding wilderness, its very hopelessness and savagery seemed to approach them nearer, to draw them gently, to look upon them, to envelop them with a solicitude irresistible, familiar, and disgusting" (OP 92). The "great silence of the surrounding wilderness" erases the sound and other elements of the West, that which embodied meaning and order for Carlier and Kayerts, leaving in their place the "void" of the wilderness (OP 81), the Western space of the station having decidedly disappeared.

With his death, Carlier's transformative journey ends prematurely, but Kayerts remains to traverse his to its conclusion. Near the story's close, Kayerts

> now found repose in the conviction that life had no more secrets for him – neither had death! ... He seemed to have broken loose from himself altogether. His old thoughts, convictions, likes and dislikes, things he respected and things he abhorred, appeared in their true light at last! Appeared contemptible and childish, false and ridiculous. He revelled in his new wisdom. (OP 97)

Kayerts' "new wisdom" is that his old thoughts and convictions, his Western values and beliefs, are now "false and ridiculous" and present nothing in their absence. At this moment, Kayerts notices the blinding mist that "had descended upon the land: the mist penetrating, enveloping, and silent" (OP 98). By appearing at the culmination of Kayerts' existential crisis, this blinding mist, this blankness without borders, represents not only the blankness of Africa but the blankness of the West. The definitive distinctions between Western and African space that Kayerts had perceived prior to his Congo experience have disappeared. He now perceives both spaces as spaces of absence. The lack of "little things," "small conveniences," "mere incidents of the surface," the "habitual" reveals for Conrad's characters the ultimate emptiness of existence, an absence that may sometimes contain contingent but never transcendent meaning. As Conrad's narrator in *Victory* concludes, "For every age is fed on illusions, lest men should renounce life early and the human race come to an end" (V 76).

Somewhat different from "An Outpost of Progress," where no respite exists from "the negation of the habitual," in *Heart of Darkness*, the "small conveniences," the "little things," the "mere incidents of the surface," the "habitual" provide some shelter from Marlow's "creepy thoughts" (HD 95), but this shelter routinely breaks down in the face of the company's brutality, disorder, inefficiency, absurdity, and "philanthropic pretence" (HD 80). In the end, such shelters prove to be mere respites when the "mere incidents of the surface" rather than the "reality" fade and the "inner truth" (previously "hidden") becomes visible. Further troubling for Marlow, whenever he confronts elements of the West in Africa they appear either out of place, absurd, or detrimental (*e.g.*, the accountant's dress (HD 70), the French gunboat "firing into a continent" (HD 65), "the grove of death" (HD 69-70)), whereas if Western civilization were the product of transcendental truths, when implemented in Africa, it would not be out of place, absurd, or detrimental.

Marlow ends by seeing Western cosmology not as a product of transcendental truths but as a construct, a social contract among Westerners, established to facilitate acceptable social interaction. He concludes that Western metaphysics, human existence, and the tactile universe are absences, that life is a "droll thing": "that mysterious of merciless logic for a futile purpose. The most you can hope from it is some knowledge of yourself – that comes too late – a crop of unextinguishable regrets" (HD 134). This discovery follows upon Marlow's "wrestle with death," where he perceives "an impalpable greyness, with nothing underfoot, with nothing around, without spectators, without clamour, without glory, without the great desire of victory, without the great fear of defeat, in a sickly atmosphere of tepid scepticism, without much belief in your own right, and still less in that of your adversary" (HD 134). Marlow's dance with death takes place in a space of negation, a negation even of sound: "I was within a hair's breadth of the last opportunity for pronouncement, and I found with humiliation that probably I would have nothing to say" (HD 134-35). Marlow's confrontation with the silent, empty space of Africa is the catalyst that carries him to this conclusion. It is during this transformation that Marlow's distinctions between a full and heterogeneous Western space and an empty and homogenous African space break down and are revealed to be "mere incidents of the surface," distinctions that are constructed not essential.

When Marlow returns to Europe, he perceives differently the same action, sound, and purpose he had encountered earlier, what had previously presented to him a heterogenous and meaningful Western space. Instead of such heterogenous and meaningful space, Marlow finds himself "resenting the sight of people hurrying through the streets" (HD 135). He complains, "They trespassed upon my thoughts. They were intruders whose knowledge of life was to me an irritating pretence, because I felt so sure they could not possibly know the things I knew" (HD 135-36). Marlow admits, "Their bearing ... which was simply the bearing of commonplace individuals going about their business in the assurance of perfect safety," but he says that their behavior "was offensive to me like the outrageous flauntings of folly in the face of a danger it is unable to comprehend." Consequently, his aunt's efforts to "'nurse up [his] strength' seemed altogether beside the mark. It was not [his] strength that wanted nursing, it was [his] imagination that wanted soothing" (HD 136). Marlow wishes, unsuccessfully, to find shelter from the pervasive absence he has uncovered.

Marlow's listeners reinforce this altered perception. When Marlow's tale concludes and he suddenly stops speaking, they have traveled their own transformative journeys. The frame narrator reveals: "Nobody moved for a time." Not only, though, are they transfixed, but they have been so engrossed that the Director reveals that they "have lost the first of the ebb" (HD 143). Furthermore, the frame narrator, who had initially shown a certain resistance to Marlow's "inconclusive" narratives (HD 55), shows in the end his own transformation, as he looks out on the Thames and sees it flowing "into the heart of an immense darkness" (HD 143). As it has for Marlow, not only England has become for the frame narrator a place of darkness but "the uttermost ends of the earth" (HD 143) are now a darkness, a homogenous dark space of negation.

Like so many of Conrad's characters who endure transformational ordeals, Marlow, having completed his Congo experience, experiences a transformation. Western space and non-Western space have become for him, his listeners, and for Conrad himself (along with perhaps even Conrad's readers), the same space: both are empty of transcendental truths; both are absolute absences. All the West's sound, activity, and heterogeneous demarcations have become for them contingent, psychological shelters imposed upon an absence. Marlow the character comes to epitomize this metaphoric journey when he returns to the West and now negates the spatial distinctions between the West and Africa in the same way that Marlow the narrator will later negate the spatial distinctions between the Thames and the Congo when he tells his tale, as both Western and non-Western spaces reveal themselves ultimately to be spaces of silence, spaces of absence.

References

Acheraïou, Amar. "Joseph Conrad's Poetics: Space and Time." *L'Epoque Conradienne*, vol. 27, 2001, pp. 33–52.

Ambrosini, Richard. *Conrad's Fiction as Critical Discourse*. Cambridge: Cambridge University Press, 1991.

Cezair-Thompson, Margaret. "The Blank Spaces in *Heart of Darkness.*" *Conradiana*, vol. 48, no. 2–3, summer-autumn 2016, pp. 169–86.

Conrad, Joseph. *Almayer's Folly*. Edited by Peter Lancelot Mallios. New York: Modern Library, 2002.

———. *Falk. Typhoon and Other Stories*. Edited by J. H. Stape. London: Penguin, 2007, pp. 119–96.

———. "Geography and Some Explorers." *Last Essays*. Edited by Harold Ray Stevens and J. H. Stape. Cambridge: Cambridge University Press, 2010, pp. 3–17.

———. *Heart of Darkness*. Edited by John G. Peters. Peterborough, Ontario: Broadview Press, 2019.

———. "Karain." *Tales of Unrest*. Edited by Allan H. Simmons and J. H. Stape. Cambridge: Cambridge University Press, 2012, pp. 13–49.

———. *Lord Jim*. Edited by Cedric Watts. Peterborough, Ontario: Broadview Press, 2001.

———. *The Nigger of the "Narcissus." The Secret Sharer and Other Stories*. Edited by John G. Peters. New York: W. W. Norton, 2015, pp. 137–254.

———. *Nostromo*. Edited by Jacques Berthoud and Mara Kalins. Oxford: Oxford University Press, 2007.

———. *An Outcast of the Islands*. Edited by Cedric Watts. London: Everyman, 1996.

———. "An Outpost of Progress." *Tales of Unrest*. Edited by Allan H. Simmons and J. H. Stape. Cambridge: Cambridge University Press, 2012, pp. 77–99.

———. *A Personal Record*. Edited by Zdzisław Najder and J. H. Stape. Cambridge: Cambridge University Press, 2008.

———. *The Rescue*. Uniform edition. Garden City, NY: Doubleday, Page, 1925.

———. *The Secret Agent*. Edited by Tanya Agathocleous. Peterborough, Ontario: Broadview Press, 2009.

———. "The Secret Sharer." *The Secret Sharer and Other Stories*. Edited by John G. Peters. New York: W. W. Norton, 2015, pp. 7–42.

———. *The Shadow-Line. The Secret Sharer and Other Stories*. Edited by John G. Peters. New York: W. W. Norton, 2015, pp. 47–135.

———. *Under Western Eyes*. Edited by John G. Peters. Peterborough, Ontario: Broadview Press, 2010.

———. *Victory*. Edited by Peter Lancelot Mallios. Modern Library, 2003.

———. "Youth: A Narrative." *Youth, Heart of Darkness, The End of the Tether*. Edited by John Lyon. London: Penguin, 1995, pp. 9–43.

Conroy, Mark. "Ghostwriting (In) 'Karain.'" *The Conradian*, vol. 18, no. 2, autumn 1994, pp. 1–16.

Dowden, Wilfred S. "The Light and the Dark; Imagery and Thematic Development in Conrad's 'Heart of Darkness.'" *Rice Institute Pamphlet*, vol. 44, no. 1, April 1957, pp. 33–51.

Fogel, Aaron. *Coercion to Speak: Conrad's Poetics of Dialogue*. Cambridge, MA: Harvard University Press, 1985.

Garnett, Edward. "Introduction." *Letters from Joseph Conrad: 1895–1924*. Edited by Edward Garnett. Indianapolis, IN: Bobbs-Merrill, 1928, pp. 1–28.

Greaney, Michael. *Conrad, Language, and Narrative*. Cambridge University Press, 2002.

Hampson, Robert. "Spatial Stories: Joseph Conrad and James Joyce." *Geographies of Modernism: Literatures, Cultures, Spaces*. Edited by Peter Brooker and Andrew Thacker. London: Routledge, 2005, pp. 55–64.

Hawthorn, Jeremy. "Blank Spaces and Hollow Men: Determinate Absences and Absent Determinants in Conrad's Fiction." *L'Epoque Conradienne*, vol. 41, 2017–18, pp. 71–83.

Howe, Irving. *Politics and the Novel*. New York: Horizon Books, 1957.

Jean-Aubry, G. *Joseph Conrad: Life and Letters*, 2 vols. Garden City, NY: Doubleday, Page, 1927.

Levin, Yael. *Joseph Conrad: Slow Modernism*. Oxford: Oxford University Press, 2020.

Lothe, Jakob. *Conrad's Narrative Method*. Oxford: Clarendon Press, 1989.

Miller, J. Hillis. *Poets of Reality: Six Twentieth Century Writers*. Cambridge: Harvard University Press, 1966.

Ross, Stephen. *Conrad and Empire*. Columbia: University of Missouri Press, 2004.

Toop, David. *Sinister Resonance: The Mediumship of the Listener*. New York: Continuum, 2010.

Watt, Ian. *Conrad in the Nineteenth Century*. Berkeley, CA: University of California Press, 1979.

West, Russell. "Space and Language in the Private Diary: Conrad's Congo Diaries." *Marginal Voices, Marginal Forms: Diaries in European Literature and History*. Edited by Rachael Langford and Russell West. Amsterdam: Rodopi, 1999, pp. 107–25.

White, Allon. *The Uses of Obscurity: The Fictions of Early Modernism*. London: Routledge & Kegan Paul, 1981.

Wollaeger, Mark A. *Joseph Conrad and the Fictions of Skepticism*. Stanford: Stanford University Press, 1990.

CHAPTER 5

Russia's Ontological Absence

Abstract Conrad considered Russia to be a non-Western space. He also saw Russia as Other both to the West and to other non-Western spaces. Unlike their engagement with Russia, as Conrad's characters engage with other non-Western spaces, they discover that the West is not founded on transcendental truths but rather on contingent truths, just as is the non-West. These characters come to recognize in the non-West and its inhabitants the ability to function effectively in a space and system different from that of the West. Russia, though, is different. Conrad saw viable alternative systems of society or values from the West in the space of Asia, Africa, and elsewhere, but he sees no such alternative system in Russia. Nor do his Russians. For Conrad, Russia lacks both transcendent and contingent truths and is instead simply a void that cannot be filled with transcendent truths nor even with contingent truths.

Keywords Joseph Conrad • Russia • Western space • Non-Western space • Absence

As noted previously, Conrad always considered Russia to be non-Western, and he reflects this state in his descriptions of a silent, empty space, at odds with the sound and fullness of the West. *The Duel* (1908), for instance, refers to "the mortal silence of the plains" and "dumb black forests" of Russia (D 167), and "The Warrior's Soul" notes of Russia that a "great

J. G. Peters, *Silence, Space and Absence in Conrad's Works*,
https://doi.org/10.1007/978-3-031-44910-9_5

winter stillness lay on the land" (WS 17). The silence of Russia is most pervasive, though, in *Under Western Eyes.* Even in his description of the city of St. Petersburg, Conrad presents a contrast between the sound and fullness of activity he describes in Western cities compared to the dominant silent and empty space that is St. Petersburg. When Razumov goes to find Ziemianitch, the streets of St. Petersburg are almost entirely silent and empty: "Along the roadway sledges glided phantom-like. … The passers-by were rare. They came upon him suddenly, looming up black in the snowflakes close by, then vanishing all at once – without footfalls" (UWE 66). Even within doors, silence pervades this city; at General T——'s home, "the silence of the room was like the silence of the grave; perfect, measureless, for even the clock on the mantelpiece made no sound" (UWE 79; see also 81, 82 and 87), and whenever St. Petersburg appears elsewhere in the novel, it appears perpetually silent and empty. Even in those instances when sound breaks the silence, the effect resembles that of Africa in *Heart of Darkness* (HD 86, 93, 107) or Asia in "Youth" (Y 40): sound bursts through a barrier of silence – but only momentarily, soon to be swallowed in a suffocating shroud of silence.

Early in *Under Western Eyes,* when two sledges collide, one of the drivers bellows, "Oh, thou vile wretch!" This "hoarse yell" "disturbed Razumov" (UWE 74) by being so out of character with the pervasive and penetrating silence he perceives of St. Petersburg. This abrupt sound, though, is soon snuffed out, as silence dominates the scene. Even more dramatic is the bombing itself: "In an instant there was a terrible shock," but the "detonation" of the first bomb is "muffled in the multitude of snowflakes" (UWE 53). The second bomb reinforces this effect; it "exploded with a terrific concentrated violence," but the Western narrator fails even to mention an accompanying sound (UWE 54). Sound of course accompanied the explosion, but Conrad's narrator notes none, emphasizing instead the absence of sound in the scene: "a solitude in the street for hundreds of yards in each direction" (UWE 54). As we have seen elsewhere in Conrad's canon, absent sound is associated with absent space, both being metonyms for a general absence: a universe of absence. This association is certainly evident in Conrad's representation of Russia.

More than this, though, Conrad represents the space of Russia as a wholly different sort of non-Western space than that found in Asia, Africa, the open ocean, and elsewhere. Ultimately, for Conrad, Russia is an entity unto itself, associated to be sure with silence but even more pervasively with absence.

Conrad famously recounted that Otto von Bismark, then Prussian Minister to Russia, is said to have stated, "*La Russie, c'est le néant*" ("Russia is a nothingness" (AW 380; my translation)). Conrad clearly concurs when he later insists in a 20 October 1911 letter to Edward Garnett: "As to discussing Russia it's the most chimeric of enterprises since it is there for anyone to look at. 'La Russie c'est le néant' Prince Bismarck said in 1864 – ... C'est le néant. Anybody with eyes can see it" (CL 4: 489). Elsewhere, Conrad argues, "Russia is bound to remain a *Néant* for many long years, in a more even than the Bismarckian sense" (AW 381), because "Russian autocracy succeeded to nothing; it had no historical past, and it cannot hope for a historical future" (AW 383). For Conrad, nothing comes from nothing.

Nor did the Russian Revolution alter Conrad's thinking. In a 6 May 1917 letter to John Quinn, Conrad remarks of Russia's role in the First World War before and after the revolution: "It counted for little – and now it counts for just nothing" (CL 6: 86), and in a later letter to Quinn, Conrad continued to contend that the "great thing is to keep the Russian infection, its decomposing power, from the social organism of the rest of the world" (6 February 1918; CL 6: 180), a "decomposing power" that Conrad undoubtedly thought would spread Russian nothingness. More telling still, in his 1920 "Author's Note" to *Under Western Eyes*, Conrad pessimistically predicted: "These people are unable to see that all they can effect is merely a change of names. The oppressors and the oppressed are all Russians together; and the world is brought once more face to face with the truth of the saying that the tiger cannot change his stripes nor the leopard his spots" (UWE 46). Russia thus remained unchanged: a nothingness before the revolution and a nothingness after.

Elsewhere as well, Conrad regularly represented Russia as an empty expanse, both in its spatial extension but also in its essence. For him, Russia was wholly Other. Despite geographical designations to the contrary, Conrad viewed Russia (unlike his native Poland) as wholly non-European, in short as non-Western; Conrad refers, for instance, to Russia exhibiting an "impenetrability to whatever is true in Western thought" (AW 383), and he asserts that "the testamentary Russia of Peter the Great – who imagined that all the nations were delivered into the hand of Tsardom – can do nothing. It can do nothing because it does not exist" (AW 377). In its space exists an emptiness, and all things Russian embody, for Conrad, both otherness and emptiness.

Although spatial emptiness has been a prominent feature of the non-Western world of Asia, Africa, the open ocean, and elsewhere, it is most prominent in Conrad's Russia. Conrad's Russian tales, "The Warrior's Soul," *The Duel*, and *Under Western Eyes*, all associate Russia with emptiness. The narrator of "The Warrior's Soul," for instance, remarks, "I had the intimate sensation of the earth in all its enormous expanse wrapped in snow, with nothing showing on it but trees with their straight stalk-like trunks and their funeral verdure; and in this aspect of general mourning I seemed to hear the sighs of mankind falling to die in the midst of a nature without life" (WS 20). And although not specifically equating the Russian expanse with emptiness, *The Duel* describes this space in similar language, referring to Russia's "white immensity" (D 168). This correlative of Russia with vast emptiness is most prominent, however, in *Under Western Eyes.* Early in the novel, through the narrator's Western eyes, Razumov "received an almost physical impression of endless space and of countless millions," experiencing what appears to be not empty space but in reality "endless space" inhabited by "countless millions"; however, the narrator then elaborates: "Under the sumptuous immensity of the sky, the snow covered the endless forests, the frozen rivers, the plains of an immense country, obliterating the landmarks, the accidents of the ground, levelling everything under its uniform whiteness" (UWE 71). The "countless millions," though extant, are also absent – buried under the blank expanse of snow.

More striking still is the space of Russia itself. After describing the "levelling" quality of Russia's "uniform whiteness," the teacher of languages paraphrases Razumov likening Russia to "a monstrous blank page" (UWE 71). Late in the novel, the narrator's Western eyes again present Razumov experiencing a similar scene, but one even more blank: "The great white desert of frozen, hard earth glided past his eyes without a sign of human habitation" (UWE 277). Although this "endless space" contains plains, people, rivers, forests, and landmarks, it is, nonetheless, a "great white desert." This insistance of blankness places Russia as the most extreme example of homogenous space, not only lacking demarcations but lacking substance altogether; all is obliterated under the snow's uniformity, leaving blankness in its stead.[1] The ubiquitous snow burying Russia in *The Duel*, "The Warrior's Soul," and *Under Western Eyes* is a blankness

[1] The snow in "The Warrior's Soul," *The Duel*, and *Under Western Eyes*, like the fog in "The Tale" (1917) (Ta 64, 67-70, 72-73, 76, 79), "An Outpost of Progress" (OP 98-99), and *Heart of Darkness* (HD 98-103), is a metaphor for blankness that erases all it envelops. This same state also exists in the darkness of the Golfo Placido in *Nostromo*: Nostromo "saw nothing but a smooth darkness, like a solid wall" (N 218; see also 188, 199, and 388). *The Shadow-Line* includes a similar scene of darkness: "If the air had turned black, the sea … might have turned solid. It was no good looking in any direction. … When the time came the blackness would overwhelm silently the bit of starlight falling upon the ship, and the end of all things would come without a sigh, stir, or murmur of any kind" (SL 119).

resembling the snow that is "general all over Ireland" (240, 250) in James Joyce's "The Dead" (1914), where, together with Conrad's Russia, it represents, both literally and metaphorically, a uniform absence of life in the land. This absence is exemplified in Razumov's later vision of Russia: even the people have disappeared from this blank space, "as if totally dehumanized" (Acheraïou 34), a blankness that suggests an emptying of all objects and demarcations lying under its uniformity and suggesting both the frozen desert of wintry death as well as its blank, homogenous whiteness. This suggestion of blankness places Russia as the most extreme example of homogenous space, not only lacking demarcations but lacking substance altogether, because counter to the blankness of the Congo, which was unexplored, the space of Russia was well traveled, and yet those travels reveal not fullness but blankness. Furthermore, although the homogeneity of the non-West (outside Russia) is a perceptual illusion, this space remains blank in one significant facet: it is (like the West) empty of transcendental truths but not of contingent truths.

Unlike the epiphanic effect resulting from the encounter with so many other non-Western spaces, the encounter with Russia is otherwise. As Conrad's characters engage with the former colonial world, they encounter a counter-narrative to the colonial narrative of cultural superiority (an inviolable part of the narrative of benefit), and this causes them to question Western cosmology. In contrast to so many Western characters who experience a transformation through their encounters with non-Western space, the Western teacher of languages experiences no such transformation. In fact, his encounter with Russia through the events of *Under Western Eyes* actually bolsters his views of Western superiority, as his "Western eyes" consistently observe the "confused immensity of the Eastern borders" (UWE 300). In effect, Russia reinforces confidence in the West by way of contrast.

Other non-Western spaces show an alternative to the monolith of Western cosmology that convinces Conrad's characters to reassess the West and conclude that Western values are contingent not transcendent. The primary difference between Russia and the rest of the non-West is that the rest of the non-West has erected contingent truths that allow such societies to facilitate effective social association. Conrad certainly did not unfailingly affirm non-Western cultures, but he often recognized that these cultures function efficiently, and he often recognized something to affirm in them, such as the cannibals' restraint in *Heart of Darkness* (HD 100-01), or the dignity of Karain's demeanor and that of Dain Maroola,

Dain Waris, Hassim, Immada, Nina Almayer, and certain other non-Westerners, or the way Malay culture accepts Nina where Western culture rejects her.

Non-Westerners in these societies also affirm their societies. Mrs. Almayer, for instance, insists that Westerners "think lies because they despise us that are better than they are" (AF 119). She sees her people as better and her culture as superior, as implicitly do Hassim and Immada in *The Rescue*, who clearly affirm their culture over the West of Mr. Travers and Mr. Shaw.

As we have seen, Karain also compares the West unfavorably to his own world. He wishes to accompany the gunrunners to the West, but only because of its absence of soul, which he believes can rid him of Matara's ghost (K 40). Were he not haunted, he would have no desire to leave his world for the West.

Babalatchi is even more direct in rejecting the West and accepting his own culture. He complains to Lingard:

> It is written that the earth belongs to those who have fair skins and hard but foolish hearts. … You are strange, you white men. You think it is only your wisdom and your virtue and your happiness that are true. You are stronger than the wild beasts, but not so wise. A black tiger knows when he is not hungry – you do not. He knows the difference between himself and those that can speak; you do not understand the difference between yourselves and us – who are men. You are wise and great – and you shall always be fools. (OI 174-75)

Babalatchi goes on to accuse the Western colonizers: "But you whites have taken all: the land, the sea, and the power to strike! And there is nothing left for us in the islands" (OI 177). Implied in Babalatchi's criticism of the ways of the West is an affirmation of his own culture, which he believes responds to the world otherwise.

Other non-Western characters exhibit a concurrent confidence in their cultures and complementary critique of the West. As a consequence of these various instances of affirmation of indigenous cultures, Conrad presents the spaces of the non-Western world offering an alternative to the West, and non-Westerners exhibit an accompanying alternative in their way of looking at the world.

Russia, however, offers nothing of the kind. It can offer no alternative to the West because for Conrad, unlike the *tabula rasa* of other non-Western spaces (and of Western spaces), no contingent truths are or can be written on the "monstrous blank page" of Russia (UWE 71). It will ever be a blank page. Russia, as truly *néant*, can offer nothing in place of the West because it is nothing. For Conrad, "under the shadow of Russian autocracy nothing could grow" (AW 383). Russia "is and has been simply the negation of everything worth living for. She is … a bottomless abyss that has swallowed up every hope of mercy, every aspiration towards personal dignity, towards freedom, towards knowledge, every ennobling desire of the heart, every redeeming whisper of conscience" (AW 385), because "*Le Néant* has been the extirpation of every intellectual hope" (AW 384). Absent contingent truths, let alone transcendent truths, to facilitate effective social interaction, Russians cannot confirm Russia. Sophia Antonovna, for example, chronicles her father's life:

> No joy had lighted up his laborious days. He died at fifty. … No protection, no guidance! What had society to say to him? Be submissive and be honest. If you rebel I shall kill you. If you steal I shall imprison you. But if you suffer I have nothing for you – nothing except perhaps a beggarly dole of bread – but no consolation for your trouble, no respect for your manhood, no pity for the sorrows of your miserable life. (UWE 238)

The Russia that Tekla experiences is a Russia where people "have nowhere to go and nothing to look forward to in this life" (UWE 157). Natalia Haldin's Russia is a Russia where reform "is impossible. There is nothing to reform. There is no legality, there are no institutions" (UWE 144). Russia is, in short, a concatenation of negation. Victor Haldin sees a Russia that destroys "the spirit and progress of truth" (UWE 61). The owner of the eating house that Ziemianich haunts concludes of Russia: "Who could bear life in our land without the bottle?" (UWE 68). Finally, Razumov comes to confront this same Russia:

> His heart had, as it were, suddenly emptied itself. It was no use struggling on. Rest, work, solitude, and the frankness of intercourse with his kind were alike forbidden to him. Everything was gone. His existence was a great cold blank, something like the enormous plain of the whole of Russia levelled with snow and fading gradually on all sides into shadows and mists. (UWE 268)

In contrast to other non-Westerners, so many of Conrad's Russians cannot confirm Russia – because there is nothing to confirm.

Ultimately, Russia differs from other non-Western spaces because, Conrad contends, it is in fact neither East nor West. Russia is "a yawning chasm open between East and West" (AW 385). Russia "has neither an

European nor an Oriental parentage; more, it seems to have no root either in the institutions or the follies of this earth. … It is like a visitation, like a curse from Heaven falling in the darkness of ages upon the immense plains of forest and steppe lying dumbly on the confines of two continents: a true desert harbouring no spirit either of the East or of the West" (AW 383). In the end, Conrad considers Russia an entity unto itself, or perhaps more accurately, an absence unto itself.

References

Acheraïou, Amar. "Joseph Conrad's Poetics: Space and Time." *L'Epoque Conradienne*, vol. 27, 2001, pp. 33–52.

Conrad, Joseph. *Almayer's Folly*. Edited by Peter Lancelot Mallios. New York: Modern Library, 2002.

———. "Author's Note" to *Under Western Eyes*. *Under Western Eyes*. Edited by John G. Peters. Peterborough, Ontario: Broadview Press, 2010, pp. 44–46.

———. "Autocracy and War." *Under Western Eyes*. Edited by John G. Peters. Peterborough, Ontario: Broadview Press, 2010, pp. 371–97.

———. *The Collected Letters of Joseph Conrad*. Edited by Laurence Davies, et al, 9 vols. Cambridge: Cambridge University Press, 1983–2008.

———. *The Duel*. *A Set of Six*. Edited by Allan H. Simmons and Michael Foster. Cambridge: Cambridge University Press, 2021, pp. 133–208.

———. *Heart of Darkness*. Edited by John G. Peters. Peterborough, Ontario: Broadview Press, 2019.

———. *An Outcast of the Islands*. Edited by Cedric Watts. London: Everyman, 1996.

———. "An Outpost of Progress." *Tales of Unrest*. Edited by Allan H. Simmons and J. H. Stape. Cambridge: Cambridge University Press, 2012, pp. 77–99.

———. *Nostromo*. Edited by Jacques Berthoud and Mara Kalins. Oxford: Oxford University Press, 2007.

———. *The Shadow-Line*. *The Secret Sharer and Other Stories*. Edited by John G. Peters. New York: W. W. Norton, 2015, pp. 47–135.

———. "The Tale." *Tales of Hearsay*. Uniform edition. Garden City, NY: Doubleday, Page, 1925, pp. 59–81.

———. *Under Western Eyes*. Edited by John G. Peters. Peterborough, Ontario: Broadview Press, 2010.

———. "The Warrior's Soul." *Tales of Hearsay*. Uniform edition. Garden City, NY: Doubleday, Page, 1925, pp. 1–26.

Joyce, James. "The Dead." *Dubliners*. Edited by Keri Walsh. Peterborough, Ontario: Broadview Press, 2016, pp. 207–51.

Index[1]

[1] Note: Page numbers followed by 'n' refer to notes.

J. G. Peters, *Silence, Space and Absence in Conrad's Works*, https://doi.org/10.1007/978-3-031-44910-9

G

H

J

K

L

M

N

P

Q

R

S

T

W

Printed in the USA
CPSIA information can be obtained
at www.ICGtesting.com
LVHW022030220324
775250LV00005B/503

9 783031 449093